D0504548

The
WRINKLIES'
ARMCHAIR COMPANION

First published in Great Britain in 2011

Prion Books
an imprint of the
Carlton Publishing Group
20 Mortimer Street
London W1T 3JW

A catalogue record for this book is available from the British
Library

ISBN 978-1-85375-820-1

Printed in the UK by CPI Group (UK) Ltd, Croydon, CR0 4YY

10 9 8 7 6 5 4 3 2

The

WRINKLIES'
ARMCHAIR COMPANION

Mike Haskins
& Clive Whichelow

Contents

Introduction   6

Chapter 1: So You've Survived Another Night   9

Chapter 2: Reasons To Stay In Today   27

Chapter 3: Let's Get Comfy   41

Chapter 4: Everything Nice And Handy   57

Chapter 5: What's On Telly, Then?   73

Chapter 6: Who The Hell's This Now? The Wrinkly's
    Guide To Visitors   85

Chapter 7: Nodding Off   99

Introduction

Now, you may be asking why exactly you need an armchair companion. You may already have a perfectly good armchair companion in the form of your silly old cat, your smelly old dog, or some other equally loveable furry mammal. You may have your wrinkly other half – who may also pass as a loveable furry mammal. You have your tin of biccies, your remote control, your favourite book and various other bits and bobs that put the 'mm' into 'comfort'.

In short, you're sorted.

But are you? The armchair is the cockpit of wrinkly cruising, the command centre of wrinkly mission control, the nuclear bunker of wrinkly world domination. With your white phone to hand for personal calls, your green phone for chats with world leaders and your red phone for international emergencies, your armchair is the epicentre of your wrinkly world. What's that? You only have one phone? Well, that's fine; it leaves more room for biccies on the coffee table. Got to get the priorities right.

But apart from your wrinkly electronic gadgets, or what the experts call 'nannytechnology', you also have to consider every eventuality that might occur while you are luxuriating in your favourite chair.

For example, do you have a decent assortment of sure-fire excuses to get rid of unwanted callers at the door? Do you know how to exercise without actually getting up? Do you have a full range of amusements to keep you going until there's something decent on the box? And that could be quite a yawning chasm to fill, if we're honest.

As you've probably worked out by now, being a wrinkly is a full-time job. Other people, of the non-wrinkly variety, may look askance at your apparently leisurely lifestyle, but they don't have a clue what's actually going on behind your ever-twitching curtains.

Yes, the curtain-twitching. Some look upon it as an anti-social activity, spying on neighbours and other folk going about their lawful business. But what they don't understand, what they can't get into their soppy, unlined heads, is that you are the third arm of the law.

There's the real police, the PCSOs and you – all standing four-square against the muggers, murderers and illegal flytippers infesting your neighbourhood. OK, so you haven't actually caught any international jewel thieves or terrorists yet, but it's only a matter of time. Oh, those suspicious neighbours will be glad of you one day.

And quite apart from helping you with your clandestine law enforcement role, *The Wrinklies' Armchair Companion* will help you to make those important daily decisions such as: cake or biscuits, tea or coffee, crustless cucumber sandwich or tuna and brie submarine melt and easy on the mayo?

Then there's the reading matter, the televisual toss-up between live TV, DVD or wonky old video. You might also want to consider the ins and outs of armchair gambling, the possibility of training your pets to fetch snacks and hot beverages, the pros and cons of inviting in doorstep salesmen, the art of vacuuming while sitting down…

There are 1001 things to consider – perhaps more. And people have the flippin' cheek to ask you what you do with yourself all day!

You also have to know the finer points of getting truly comfy. There are probably whole branches of ancient Eastern thought dedicated to the art of cushion-plumping, acres of arcane print listing a hundred and one ways to relax (the Calmer Sutra, probably), and phalanxes of mystics and yogis who could coach you in the science of comfology.

Of course, to get truly comfy you need peace and quiet, and that's something that's not easy to come by in the migraine-inducing modern world.

If it's not noisy neighbours with their dreadful so-called

music blaring out of extra-loud speakers, or road drills thrumming away at all hours of the day and night, it's barking dogs, barking-mad passers-by, election vans, ice-cream men, people learning how to play the drums (how is it you never hear someone who's actually learnt to play the drums?), police sirens, babies, feral foxes... it's enough to make you scream (quietly, of course).

Then there's the 'S' word. Sleep. Nodding off. Forty winks. Resting your eyes.

No self-respecting wrinkly is going to admit in public that they need to sleep in the day, but as we have already established, wrinklydom is a hard taskmaster and it can take it out of you.

In this book, then, you will find tips on how to grab that extra bit of shut-eye without offending your guests or, conversely, how to use the strategic snooze to get rid of them.

There is also a wrinkly list of things that are almost guaranteed to set the poor old eyelids drooping.

So this will be the handbook that guides you through the waking indoor day, the Who's Who of visitors, the What's What of wrinkly home comforts, the dictionary of dossing, the encyclopaedia of inertia...

In a nutshell, it's *The Wrinklies' Armchair Companion*. Never venture to your armchair without it!

Mike Haskins and Clive Whichelow

Chapter 1:
So You've Survived
Another Night

There's only one thing worse than waking up and finding you're a wrinkly, and that's not waking up at all.

So, if you've woken up this morning, well done, congrats, and please can you let us know the secret of your longevity?

Lord knows you've had some close shaves over the past 24 hours. You've successfully negotiated the most treacherous reaches of the most dangerous place on earth – i.e. your own house.

Yes, it's been statistically proven that most accidents happen in the home, and you may be forgiven for thinking that the majority of accidents happen in your home.

What with dopey cats sleeping on the stairs and small, strategically placed objects left by grandchildren impeding your smooth transition from one room to another, plus the inherent dangers left in the wake of your feeble attempts at DIY, it's amazing that you've lived this long.

And we haven't even mentioned the kitchen. If ever a household room vied with the burning fires of hell for potential disaster and misery it would be the kitchen.

From burning hot oven rings left on by someone whose memory was last seen floating down the Suwannee (not your own, of course) to chip pans with minds of their own and banana skins literal and metaphorical, the kitchen has long been the undoing of many a wrinkly.

There should be a sign on the door reading 'Here Be Monsters'. But unfortunately there's just one reading 'City Of Westminster: Gentlemen's Toilets.'

In fact it's probably only your sense of humour that's kept you going.

First, you couldn't sleep last night because you kept hearing strange noises. Finally, after a couple of hours debating whether to go downstairs armed with the poker that you suddenly remembered was sent to the charity shop in 1975, you realized that all the strange noises were coming from your own stomach.

Then, when you did finally drop off, next door's teenage offspring rolled home from a night's clubbing to disturb your beauty sleep with slamming taxi doors and drunken renditions of the complete works of Kylie Minogue.

When you did eventually get off, it seemed like the slightest bat of a gnat's eyelid before you were wide awake again with your poor old wrinkly bladder imploring you to visit the lavatory.

Barely had you slipped one gnarled old leg back under the duvet before your wrinkly other half said, 'Making the tea, then?'

And we haven't even touched on those terrifying dreams about the Chancellor of the Exchequer smiling his evil Sardonicus smile and frittering away your pension, or the cat and mouse playing, well, cat-and-mouse in your kitchen, or any of the other nocturnal nuisances that kept you from the land of Nod.

Nice to have you with us!

Worst Things To Hear First Thing In The Morning

It's a shame this section is only one page long, because quite frankly the list of things you don't want to hear FTITM is longer than one of Twizzle's arms.

So let's narrow it down to a top 15:

1. It's your turn to make the tea.
2. The winter fuel allowance has been abolished.
3. The dustmen are on strike.
4. I've just noticed that your important doctor's appointment was yesterday.
5. We've run out of milk.
6. The newspaper boy's left the wrong paper again – the FT.
7. It's snowing!
8. The alarm clock must be playing up – it's only ten past three.
9. Our cat's got a bird in the kitchen.
10. Our grandson's got a bird in the club.
11. A road drill outside your house.
12. A neighbour calling 'Cooee!' through the letterbox.
13. A team of policemen battering down your front door in the (probably) mistaken belief that it is in fact a crack den.
14. The radio playing 'The Birdie Song'.
15. Your other half playing back the tape they've made of you snoring.

We have left a short space here for you to fill in your own:

How You Rationalized All Those Things That Went Bump In The Night

The first thing to consider is: why don't things go bump in the day? This immediately turns the wrinkly mind to thoughts of conspiracy, i.e. things don't just go bump in the night all by themselves; it's someone trying to get your goat.

And your goat, quite frankly, is almost permanently off the leash these days, waiting to be got by almost anyone who happens by. It works, you may well believe, something like this:

Burglars

At 3.00am you are awoken by a loud bump downstairs. The first thing that comes to mind is 'burglar'. At 3.00am the rational wrinkly mind is not fully functioning so you don't stop to wonder why a burglar should make one solitary bump, unless he's fallen down the chimney like a felonious Father Christmas.

Your second thought may well be something along the lines of: 'I'll go downstairs with a blunt instrument and teach that so-and-so a lesson he won't forget.'

Your third thought will possibly be: 'Unless we're experiencing a bizarre localized geriatric crime wave, he's going to be younger than me, and probably fitter, so perhaps I'll stay in bed a bit longer and just listen out to see what happens next.'

If another bump comes, the wrinkly either starts fumbling in the dark for a blunt instrument or tries to rationalize what else the noise could be. And this is where the conspiracy theories come in.

Conspiracy theories

You remember you still have the lawnmower you borrowed from next door three months ago. Being British, and wrinkly, your neighbours are far too polite to mention it, so they get up at 3.00am and make burglar noises to keep you awake, so that in your paranoid state your fevered mind will whisk through all the anxieties and lumps of guilt that are cluttering up your wrinkly brain.

After some thought, you realize this is plainly ridiculous, especially as you recall that you actually gave the lawnmower back last Thursday, which, in wrinkly memory terms, is around the turn of the last ice age.

Other explanations

The wrinkly mind then turns to other explanations for the nocturnal knock. It's the cat. Lucky you didn't go down with the blunt instrument and reduce the cat's longevity to a mere eight lives. But you haven't got a cat, you remember – it shuffled off this mortal coil four years ago.

The floorboards. Of course. As the heating switches itself off at 10.30pm, the floorboards begin to slowly expand (or is it contract?) and emit eerie Hammer House of Horror-style creaks and groans that will send shivers up the spine of all but the hardiest of wrinklies. Shiver me timbers indeed!

But it's 3.00am, you think. Surely any expanding (or contracting) should have finished by now?

Then there's the explanation of last resort: 'Perhaps I imagined it?'

Yes, that'll do. And from then on you sleep like a baby.

Nocturnal Stumbling In The Dark

Yes, all things considered, it's something of a miracle that you ever reach your armchair in the morning.

Quite apart from the nerve-jangling hunts for non-existent burglars in the middle of the night, the wrinkly has other reasons to stumble around in the dark at all hours.

Firstly, and fairly obviously, there is the trip, or possibly trips plural, to the smallest room, usually at some unearthly hour which glares out accusingly at you from the display on your digital alarm clock, for example: 3.57am.

You have a brief argument with yourself, or more pertinently with your bladder:

You: Can't you hang on for another three hours?
Your bladder: No, I can't. Twenty minutes, tops.'
You: Oh, all right then. But I don't want to have to do this again before 7.00am at the earliest.
Your bladder: I'll do my best, but I can't promise anything.

So off you go, tripping over your slippers, trying to find the door handle by memory alone, feeling your way along the landing and crashing over vacuum cleaner brushes, bags of freshly-bought toiletries and various other encumbrances along the way. It's not called a 'trip' to the loo for nothing, you know.

Men then need to engage in precision peeing to find the microscopic no-man's-land between bowl rim and water in order to make the minimum noise. It is 3.57am or so, after all.

After years of practice, men have got no better at this and either make a noise like Niagara Falls in the rainy season or, even worse, fail to realize that the toilet seat has been down all along (note to self: must put bifocals on before leaving bedroom).

Female wrinklies have it slightly easier. The homing

device located in the wrinkly posterior will find the loo without too much problem, the only danger being that the male wrinkly has been in half an hour before and splashed the seat.

How can all this be avoided? The wrinkly knows better than to drink hot beverages after about 8.30pm, and to use the loo immediately before lights out, but to no avail. The wrinkly bladder has a mind of its own and will have its wrinkly host jumping in and out of bed like a footballer throughout the hours of darkness. Which might be why they are known as the wee small hours.

But, burglars and loo visits aside, you may also be called from your bed by the cat crying to either go out or come in.

Or you will suddenly sit bolt-upright in bed at, perhaps, 2.52am, with the sudden thought that you have left the oven on. This necessitates a nocturnal stumble of a magnitude that probably requires Sherpa guides.

Not only do you have to negotiate the landing with all its obstacles and dangers, but also the stairs, hallway and other points south.

On arrival, naturally, the oven is resolutely off.

You are simultaneously both satisfied and peeved.

The Perilous Journey From Bed To Armchair

You would think, wouldn't you, that getting from your bed to your armchair would be a simple, hassle-free process, but oh no, there are myriad dangers, disasters and all manner of other terrible things beginning with 'd' to consider.

Clutter round the bed

In theory, there's a home for everything in the bedroom: shoes in the wardrobe, books on the bedside table, your wrinkly other half in bed beside you... But in practice, the bedroom is cluttered to a degree that would give a Feng Shui expert palpitations. Before you even get out of bed you are in mortal danger of multiple scalds when your other half brings you a welcome cup of early-morning tea, slips on the rug by your bedside and jettisons the entire contents of said cup over your expectant wrinkly face.

Right tangles

When you gaily swing your feet out of bed on to the floor you risk tangling one foot in the sheets, thereby performing a sort of semi-recumbent version of the splits that would bring smiles of admiration and envy from a Russian Olympic gymnast.

Trouser traumas

The simple act of putting on your expandable-waist slacks requires a considerable degree of concentration and physical dexterity and is quite frankly a Herculean task for a wrinkly who was away in the Land of Nod just minutes ago.

A *close shave*

For wrinkly men, even the simple act of shaving one's face is a task that is fraught with danger. Squinting into a steamed-up mirror *sans* bifocals and wielding a razor can result in an orgy of blood-letting that would shock Quentin Tarantino.

Stairway to Heaven

You may be one of those lucky (and very sensible) wrinklies who lives in a bungalow, but pity those poor souls who have to negotiate the wrinkly equivalent of a white-knuckle ride every morning of their lives – the stairs.

Teetering gingerly at the top with only a few yards of carpet between you and oblivion, you grab the handrail for dear life and start to put one foot in front of the other. Somehow, the degree of concentration required for this task empties your brain of any learned experience of stair-descending.

Add to this the swinging rope belt from your dressing gown that has mysteriously unravelled itself, and the loosely fitting slippers, fluffy or otherwise, and you have what will be referred to as a 'recipe for disaster' at your inquest.

Even if you are fully dressed, having negotiated the donning of comfort slacks successfully, you may well still be in a state of what the experts call 'dawn doziness', which could be enough on its own to render you incapable of getting to the breakfast table in one piece.

The final hurdle

Ah, yes: the breakfast table. Strictly speaking, that's a subject for another section of this book, but suffice it to say that your journey is only halfway over and you have yet to encounter the horrors that await through the kitchen door…

Symptoms That Wrinklies Shouldn't Worry About Too Much First Thing In The Morning

Symptom	Possible Explanation
Waking up not breathing	Not breathing is probably a very wise move owing to the build-up of noxious gases in the wrinkly bedroom over night, especially if the window has been left closed.
Waking up with your heart not beating	When wrinklies relax in bed at night, they can really relax. This may even extend to the wrinkly heart stopping working. Wrinklies, of course, never draw attention to such minor medical problems and usually carry on as normal in the hope that the heart will restart itself at some point during the morning. After all, why else do so many wrinklies choose to start the day with a strong cup of coffee?
No sign of brain activity	Well, what do you expect after five hours watching what was on telly last night?
Your life flashing before your eyes	Wrinklies often think they see all the scenes from their life flashing before their eyes in rapid succession first thing in the morning. You should not worry, however. It is not a hallucination. That was your life.
Your family gathered round your bed, sobbing	Again, no cause for concern – it may just be because none of them has ever cared for your choice in duvet covers.
Defibrillator pads placed on chest	Try not to worry. Just look on it as a jump start first thing on a chilly morning.
Waking up in wooden box	OK. Maybe now's a good time to start worrying.

Mornings: The Best Time Of Day For Wrinklies

- If wrinklies get up early and start moving round quickly enough they can get quite a lot done before their wrinkly bodies remember how painful and stiff they feel all the time.

- Now the world is bathed in bright sunlight, wrinklies can just about see what they're doing again.

- Early morning is a great time for wrinklies to stand talking loudly outside the homes of any neighbour who woke them up in the early hours of the morning and who is now lying in bed with a hangover.

- After sitting through the same stories over and over again in all the previous day's news bulletins, the morning brings a fresh range of terrible, appalling and enraging news stories for wrinklies to enjoy.

- Wrinklies can look forward to the post arriving in the morning – and now that the post doesn't arrive until lunchtime, this gives wrinklies even longer to look forward to it each day and less time afterwards to feel disappointed that the post all turned out to be advertising mailshots and things addressed to the previous owners of the house.

- Each morning wrinklies awake with a renewed sense of purpose and determination and carefully prepare a detailed list of all the things they are going to put off till tomorrow or get their wrinkly partners to do.

- Young people are all still asleep – mornings therefore represent an opportunity for wrinklies to stage a bloodless coup and retake control of the country.

Kitchen Catastrophes You've Avoided

The kitchen is the culinary equivalent of downtown Beirut. You could go in there a happy and contented wrinkly and come out... well, on a stretcher probably.

So watch out for the following:

- Scalding hot hobs.
- Daft domestic pets liable to spring across your path at any moment.
- Puddles of slippery chip fat underfoot.
- Sharp instruments.
- Boiling, bubbling liquids.
- A range of volatile electrical equipment, and indeed, the quite terrifying and ever-present mix of water and electricity.

Not to mention food past its sell-by date, salmonella, food poisoning, *E. coli* and numerous other food-related terrors.

Then there are toasters that seem primed to pop up the toast just as you are peering down at close quarters to ascertain how much bloody longer it's going to take, and nearly have your eye out.

The smoke alarm reminds you that you once read that 77% of household blazes are caused by chip pan fires. It also reminds you that you still have to get a new battery for the smoke alarm and have been meaning to do so for five and a half months. Ever since you read about the 77% of household fires, in fact.

That old standby of many a black and white comedy film, the banana skin, may be lurking round any corner waiting to spring.

Coiled like an anaconda and disguising itself as a floor tile, it awaits your slippered foot like a jungle predator.

Even if you don't eat bananas, you still worry that one may have slithered in through the cat flap or something. The only answer is permanent vigilance.

And those sell-by dates – they're not very wrinkly-friendly, are they? You know how council literature these days is printed in 43 languages and gives you the option of a Braille version? Well, what we really need is a version in Wrinklese – i.e. very large letters.

Same with sell-by dates. It's all very well for young whippersnappers to be saved from certain death by eating a yoghurt two weeks past its sell-by, but what about us wrinklies? That's probably why the mortality rate among wrinklies is far higher than that among teenagers.

Then you've got sharp instruments. Wrinklies, like everyone else, test the sharpness of a knife by running a finger along the sharp edge. If this method draws blood they exclaim, 'Ooh! That's sharp!' If it doesn't, they run their finger along the sharp edge again a bit harder. This explains the well-known oxymoron 'human intelligence'.

Apart from sharp knives, there are potato-peelers, cheese graters, large two-pronged forks and, horrors of horrors, electrically assisted spinning blades, otherwise known as food mixers.

No-one would be daft enough to put their fingers into a food mixer to test the sharpness of the blades, would they? No: but it has been known for a wrinkly to forget to put the lid on, thereby redecorating the kitchen walls and ceiling with home-made vegetable soup.

Nocturnal Nuisance Neighbours

So, you got out of the kitchen in one piece, but was your beauty sleep disturbed last night by the above-mentioned nocturnal nuisance neighbours?

Wrinklies, as you can personally attest, lead very quiet lives. This may be partly due to the fact that their hearing is not what it once was.

However, even the hardest of hearing would probably hear the dreadful thump-thump-thump of next door's 'music' at 3.00am.

Even deaf people would feel the vibrations of the bass reverberating through their body like some fiendish James Bond sonic weapon.

Perhaps this is one of the reasons why the wrinkly's hearing is not quite up to muster these days. After a lifetime of sonic onslaught by thundering traffic, execrable so-called music, road drills and all the rest, the lengthening lugholes have finally given up the ghost. You can't blame them. They've thrown in the towel and said, 'I quit.'

Drums may be there to be beaten, but eardrums should be left alone.

And why is it that some neighbours (no names mentioned) wait until the small hours of the morning to start making a racket?

What normal person suddenly decides at 1.30am to do a bit of hoovering? What individual in their right mind would select a similarly unearthly hour to engage in a spot of DIY that involved hammering, drilling and sawing?

But, of course, we're not talking about 'normal' people; we're talking about your neighbours. Yes, those of the constantly barking dog.

How is it, by the way, that dogs never get sore throats: never lose their voices? In fact, what he's probably barking at the top of his voice is something along the lines of, 'For Pete's sake, turn down the flipping music, put the Black & Decker away and go to bloody bed!'

Ah, if only. What you probably need to do is make a list of things you don't want to hear in the middle of the night and pop it through your neighbours' letterbox, e.g:

- Slamming car doors (unless it's the police coming to get them to turn the noise down).

- Noisy lovemaking (the thought that they're not only making an unearthly racket but also enjoying it is frankly just too much).

- Drilling. No-one has to drill at 3.00am – even if they're a 24-hour emergency dentist.

- Ridiculously loud TV. Some people these days have TV systems that are probably only marginally smaller than Screen Five of your local multiplex cinema. Often involving several loudspeakers for a 'surround sound' effect, these can give the bewildering impression that a blade-thrashing helicopter is just about to come down your chimney.

- Running up and down the stairs. People are not meant to run up and down the stairs. This is why they invented stairlifts.

- Rap, heavy metal, 'dance music'. These were not invented to be listened to, but to blast out at other people for the sole purpose of annoying them.

Mind-Crumbling Breakfast Decisions

In his book *Future Shock*, Alvin Toffler coined the term 'overchoice', meaning the bewildering number of choices of product available to the consumer. This might include, for example, having to choose between 43 flavours of yoghurt at the supermarket. The term could be used to describe the mind-boggling choices available to the average wrinkly at the breakfast table.

If the world is your oyster, then the kitchen is your Great Barrier Reef – teeming with exotic colours and shapes, some barely dreamed of.

Once upon a time the wrinkly's choice of breakfast would have been either cornflakes or no cornflakes. These days even the humble cornflake comes in sugary, nutty, crunchy and myriad other varieties, not to mention plain ol' plain.

The egg menu alone could be:

Brown	White	Free-range	Battery
Small	Medium	Large	Duck
Scrambled	Poached	Fried	Curried
Soft-boiled	Hard-boiled	W/soldiers	On toast

This would be bad enough at any time of day, but first thing in the morning?

Most of us wrinklies like a quiet life: a simple life. What we don't want is to stumble into the kitchen bleary-eyed and have to make a range of decisions that would leave Barack Obama reeling.

Just opting for toast leads to further complications. For example, butter or marge? This week butter is deemed by 'experts' to be a major cause of several deadly illnesses; last week it was margarine. Picking one or the other is akin to playing Russian Roulette every morning.

And then do you go for jam, marmalade, peanut butter, chocolate spread or perhaps something really exotic like maple syrup or Gentleman's Relish?

Choosing jam would involve running through 99 varieties, from Andorran Apple to Zimbabwean Ugli fruit. Even choosing marmalade isn't so simple any more. It can't just be a jar of orange stuff with bits of orange peel in any longer. It's thick-cut, thin-cut, Olde English, lime, lemon and, who knows, maybe even Zimbabwean Ugli fruit too.

The only answer for a breakfast-befuddled wrinkly is to have the same thing every day. Then one can go on to automatic pilot and avoid hacking through thickets of indecision, whether half-asleep or not. But what 'same thing' every day?

Full English? Too much hassle and too much artery aggro.

Porridge (or porage, if you must)? Wrinkly life is already quite enough like prison without rubbing it in.

Toast? See 'full English' above. Cornflakes? Ditto.

Pancakes? Unless it's Shrove Tuesday, we wrinklies don't do pancakes, thank you very much. Ghastly American import!

Bacon sarnie? Nice idea, but then we're back to overchoice again: back, streaky, smoked, unsmoked…

Probably the only answer is to wait for your wrinkly other half to make breakfast and leave all the decision making up to them.

OK. So that's the food side of things sorted, but what about beverages? If your nearest and dearest is busy devilling kidneys or whatever, you will be expected to at least put the kettle on.

Tea or coffee? Lapsang, Earl Grey or English Breakfast? Colombian, Kenyan or Blue Mountain? Fresh or instant?

Tea bags or tea leaves? Perhaps green tea, as it's healthier, or decaffeinated coffee? Cappuccino or Americano? Black or white? Sugar or sweetener? Cream or milk? Skimmed, semi-skimmed or more artery aggro?

When you think about it, it's amazing that the average wrinkly ever gets through breakfast. And so far we've only been through the comestible considerations.

What do you read at the breakfast table? The Times, Star, FT or the back of the cereal packet...?

Do you listen to Radio 1, 2, 3 or 4? Shock jocks or shipping forecasts? Perhaps you prefer breakfast TV? And do you have it on in the kitchen and eat at a table like civilized people or do you take a tray into the front room and eat it off your lap, not giving a fig what the neighbours might think if they could see you now?

Do you eat breakfast in your pyjamas (sounds a bit messy) or do you dress first?

After all this you may be feeling rather exhausted. You know what you need? A lie down. Yes, go back to bed. Clear your mind. Then get up and try to decide what to have for lunch.

Chapter 2:
Reasons To Stay In Today

Well, where shall we start?

We wrinklies usually need little or no excuse to stay at home. By our time of life we've probably left our homes and ventured into the outside world on many occasions. Invariably we have chosen to return home again.

We've been out but now we've come back to our own domiciles where we are nice and warm and comfy. What does that tell you?

Our entire lives are based around the idea of going home. If we go out to work, we spend all day at work looking forward to the moment we can leave and go back home again. If we have retired, we are filled with pity for those who have to leave their homes each day to go out to work.

If we go out to the shops, the only purpose of our trip is to find something that we require in order to improve the quality of our life back at home.

If we go out for a walk or some other form of exercise, the main reason for the activity will be to justify having a nice cup of tea and a biscuit when we get home again.

No wrinkly has ever gone on any holiday to any location, no matter how luxurious or exotic, without saying immediately on their return: 'Aaah! There's no place like home!' Furthermore, there is no sector of society for whom we feel such pity as the homeless.

Even if we go out for the evening, we spend the entire time trying to work out with our wrinkly spouse how soon we can slip away without seeming rude and what excuse we can give our hosts to justify our leaving.

Yes, we wrinklies have been outside, we've seen what the world has to offer and we've decided that the attractions of the external environment are often much exaggerated.

Outside it is cold, it is wet, there is dog poo on the pavement, there are all manner of ruffians and scoundrels waiting to do terrible things to us and toilets are not always handily situated. Isn't it better to stay at home?

Even the outside of the house is less inviting than the inside. Wrinklies' houses often show signs of decay on the outside, while on the inside they don't seem to have changed much in decades. Isn't that pretty much the same way a wrinkly feels?

As we get older and wrinklier our bodies even start to conspire with our natural inclination not to go out, and may eventually make us so physically decrepit that we can't leave our homes even if we want to.

Besides, if you really want to see what it's like outside these days, you can just look out of the window, or even switch on the TV or computer.

So together with home shopping and telephone banking, surely that about wraps it up for the outside world once and for all?

You Know You Didn't Really Want To Leave Your House Today When...

- You tell people you have to wait in today in case of an unexpected visit from the Jehovah's Witnesses.

- Your plumber offers to give you a definite time when he will call round and you tell him not to worry.

- You notice you have put all your clothes in the wash – even the ones you haven't been wearing.

- You ask the people whom you've arranged to go out and meet to come to yours instead – even when it's an entire school reunion.

- You find you are happy to pay the charge for the supermarket to deliver your shopping to your door, even though all you wanted was one small sachet of cat food.

- You wrap up something you already own and tell people it's a parcel for which you had to wait in all day.

- You try to get out of your appointment with the dentist by posting off your false teeth in a Jiffy bag.

- You ask the hospital if they can send your hip replacement round so your wrinkly spouse can try fitting it using a spanner and a Black & Decker Workmate.

- You claim your parents have grounded you ever since they found out you were putting them in a nursing home.

- You decide to just finish off some leftovers for your dinner – even though they're the cat's.

Things You'll Find Outside Your Home And Why They're Best Avoided

Weather

Since the dawn of time, this has been one of the main things driving people to construct shelters or houses for themselves. Inside your house you should not be troubled by weather conditions, unless of course your roof is in a particularly bad state.

Weather is, however, a particular problem for wrinklies. Wrinklies' facial features are often described by others as appearing 'weathered', if not 'shrivelled'. These are indeed the effects that will be caused by the exposure of the bare skin of the face to harsh weather conditions. Wrinklies look as wrinkly as they do because they have spent many long, hard years venturing forth in all types of weather – either trekking across the North Pole or just going to the shops for a pint of milk and a newspaper.

Over the years weather conditions have caused deeply etched wrinkles to develop. These wrinkles form naturally to act as channels through which lashing rain can travel and easily drain off the wrinkly's face. Stand next to a wrinkly on a wet day and you will notice this natural guttering system in action, with water cascading from the wrinkled face in all directions like a magnificent Roman fountain.

While wrinklies' faces have adapted to weather conditions over the years, just a little bit more exposure may now prove disastrous and going out in bad weather may finally cause the wrinkled features to dissolve completely.

Other people

Since the dawn of time this has been the other main reason driving people to construct shelters or houses for themselves. There's a reason why the front door has a lock on it, and that is to keep other people out.

Yes, your home is your castle and that means one thing: other people are the enemy. As with all castle invaders, other people need to be kept out at all costs and if they come round to visit, you are within your rights to pour boiling oil over them from the window above.

Outside the wrinkly house can be found hordes of criminals, ruffians and ne'er-do-wells whom wrinklies would want to avoid at all cost. And that's before we've even got on to people trying to sell you things or conducting surveys.

Wrinklies will only admit certain categories of people into their homes: people to whom they are married, people to whom they have given birth, people by whom they were given birth (who will need a bit of a help getting up the front step) and people whom they have known for at least several decades back into the previous millennium. Entry may not always be guaranteed even for these categories of person depending on mood, prevailing weather conditions and the time of day at which they arrive.

Otherwise, only those carrying laminated cards proving their identity and the name and address of their employer will be allowed through the wrinkly's porch (or passport control, as it is often termed).

Nature

Nature is another thing found outside the wrinkly home and which is best avoided.

Nature is lovely if you just get to watch it on the telly with Kate Humble standing in front of it. Nature then seems to be full of furry and feathery little fellows stuffing food into their cute little babies.

If, however, you make the mistake of leaving your house and immersing yourself in nature, you will not last long. Then you will quickly discover that nature is not only red in tooth and claw but quite smelly too.

Wild beasts wanting to eat you from the outside inwards and deadly bacteria wanting to eat you from the inside outwards – that's nature for you.

Yes, you may enjoy hanging out a lump of suet to be pecked by the birdies in your back garden. You should not, however, regard these creatures as your little friends who feel eternal gratitude for your donations of cold lumps of fat.

If they were just a bit bigger and had slightly sharper beaks, it would surely be a toss-up for them whether to peck apart the lump of suet left on the bird table or the larger lump of suet on legs that comes out and puts it there.

The real entertainment value of watching TV presenters standing in front of lots of nature is therefore surely waiting to see if they are suddenly unexpectedly trampled or consumed by the wild animals on whom they have foolishly turned their backs.

Dog poo

There's lots of this on the roads and pavements that lie outside the wrinkly house, and disgusting it is too. In their youth, wrinklies may have enjoyed playing a game of avoiding treading on the cracks when they skipped down the pavement. Now it's a constant and slightly more tense game of avoiding treading on something else beginning with 'cr...'.

Why can't dog-owners clear this mess up? For wrinklies there's a real danger that they will take one step on to the pavement and find themselves slithering all the way to the shops on a slippery ski run made entirely of dog poo.

Uncouth language

This is another thing that will assail you as soon as you step out of your front door, and it may not even be as a result of slipping on a dog poo just outside your gate (see above). All passers-by outside your house seem to communicate in a different language – and it's bad language.

Things you don't own

Unless you happen to be a vastly wealthy landowner or the king or queen of wherever you happen to live, once you leave your front door you will enter a world in which you don't own any of the things around you.

Things in this strange outside world will therefore probably not be to your taste and will not have been kept in as a good state of repair as all your own rubbish back at home.

Why Wrinklies Are Unsuited To Outdoor Conditions

- Wrinklies will be best preserved if they are kept in a protective environment at a constant temperature – just like all other valuable antiques.

- Wrinkly ladies tend to have carefully sculpted hairstyles. Wrinkly men also tend to have carefully sculpted hairstyles, although these are usually carefully sculpted in order to cover an ever-increasing area of shiny, bare scalp with an ever-decreasing amount of hair. For both wrinkly men and ladies, a sudden gust of wind can therefore result in instantaneous disaster.

- Similarly, wrinkly ladies' faces may often be carefully and intricately painted. Making them go outside in the rain would be a bit like putting the Mona Lisa through a car wash.

- It's easier for wrinklies to get lost if they go outside. It may also, of course, be possible for wrinklies to get lost if they stay inside, but at least there will be fewer places to look for them.

- If a wrinkly has to wrap up warm to go outside, the weight of necessary clothing may be so great that the wrinkly will be left unable to stand up or get to the door.

- For obvious reasons, as wrinklies age they become less well suited to direct sunlight and are best viewed in increasingly dark interior environments, and eventually in complete blackness. Even just throwing open the curtains to let in the sunlight on certain wrinklies will result in something resembling the final scene in *Dracula*.

The Indoor And Outdoor Weather Forecast For Wrinklies

Outdoor	Indoor
Freezing showers everywhere	Nice warm shower in bathroom as long as no-one else in the house switches a tap on while you're in there.
Howling cold gales	Howling cold gale in hallway until you put the sausage dog-shaped draught excluder across the bottom of the front door.
Ice	Ice confined to the top bit of the fridge and spouse's feet during night-time.
Mist	Mist in kitchen only when the kettle fails to switch itself off automatically.
Snow shower	Effect of snow shower only when spouse gives their hair a good brush after too many days without using Head and Shoulders.
Poor visibility	Only occurs at home when you can't remember where you put your glasses down.
Frosty outlook	Occurs at home if wrinkly partner has burnt your dinner, stayed out too late, forgotten your anniversary etc.
Thunder and lightning	Slightly dangerous to try and replicate within the home but a pretty similar effect can be achieved when a rumble of annoyance accompanies the fuse box blowing.
Warm front	Achievable at home if a wrinkly stands in front of the fire in the living room for a bit too long.

Evidence That Wrinklies Prefer To Stay Indoors Even If They Have To Go Out

Caravans

Even when a wrinkly leaves their house to go somewhere far away, they often decide to attach a miniature house to the back of their car and tow it along behind them. They can then arrive in some wild, beautiful spot far from civilisation and go and sit in their little tow-along home to have a cup of tea.

Umbrellas

If a wrinkly can't stay in their house with a roof to protect them from the elements, they will instead go out carrying a miniature extendable canvas roof on a stick.

Hats

Portable roofs that fit directly on the wrinkly's head. These are often designed with a primitive form of guttering running round the edge, known as a brim.

Conservatories

Wrinklies often have these built at the back of their houses. Conservatories are rooms made entirely from windows and are an attempt by wrinklies to provide a means of sitting out in the back garden without having to actually go outside in order to do so. Unfortunately, the conservatories are usually so big they take up the entire back garden. This leaves wrinklies sitting in their conservatories wondering where their garden has gone to and why their conservatory door is so close to the back fence that it won't open.

Indoor plants

Another attempt by wrinklies to trick themselves into believing they have ventured outside when this is not in fact the case.

Modern Stuff Available To Help Wrinklies Avoid Ever Leaving Their Homes

Telephone banking

You can now manage all your finances over the telephone as long as you can remember various passwords and secret bits of information. So it's a bit like phoning up and doing a little quiz, but the only thing on offer as a prize is your own money.

Google Earth

This allows you to spend hours travelling down every road in every continent from the comfort of your own home. It's as though all your snooping through the curtains at the neighbours has been done for you, but Google had done it on every single house everywhere in the world.

Daytime telly

When wrinklies were young, there were only two or three television stations that broadcast for just a few hours each day. Now there are hundreds of stations broadcasting all the time. Unfortunately, however, they only have enough decent programmes between them to fill two or three stations broadcasting for just a few hours each day.

Online shopping

These days it is possible to purchase anything you want online. Unfortunately, this doesn't mean that it will ever actually be delivered to you. Most online stores offer a very simple process. You only have to put your credit card details in once and the details will be available to people all over the world.

More Telltale Signs You Didn't Really Want To Go Out Today

- You phone in sick to try and get out of a doctor's appointment.

- You cancel your appointment at the hairdresser's because you say you have to stay in and wash your hair.

- You tell the garage you can't get round to them today because your car's broken down.

- You ask the members of your outdoor activities group if they'd like to come round to your house today for a change.

- You say you can't attend today's meeting of the local naturist group because you have nothing to wear.

- You say you can't meet up with your jogging group tonight because you've got the runs.

- You claim you can't get out of the house because your front door is only working in one direction.

- You tell people you've waited in all day for the doorbell repairman to come but so far you've heard nothing from him.

- You say you can't make this week's meeting of the local agoraphobia society because the room they've booked is too big.

- You say you can't make this week's meeting of the local claustrophobia society because the hall is too full of agoraphobics.

You say you didn't get to your evening class on map-reading because you got lost on the way.

The Wrinkly's Step-by-Step Guide To Doing Your Supermarket Shopping Online

1. Go to your favourite supermarket's website; alternatively, choose a supermarket as far away from your house as possible so you get the best possible value for the delivery charge they make.

2. Log in to the site by entering your password.

3. Spend half an hour trying to remember your password from the time you last attempted this 18 months ago.

4. Spend another half an hour trying to work out how to get the supermarket to send you a reminder of your password.

5. Receive an email from the supermarket reminding you that your password is the word 'password'.

6. Your supermarket's website will now appear laid out a bit like a real supermarket, but with fewer mothers shouting at their children and people standing right in front of the products you want to buy.

7. Use the drop-down menus to find the products you want. Click on them and enter the quantity required.

8. Realize the '1' button on your keyboard is still a bit sticky from the orange juice you spilt on it last week and as a result you have just ordered 1,111,111,111,111 tins of spaghetti hoops.

9. Amend the quantity or resign yourself to the fact that you will be eating nothing but spaghetti hoops for the rest of your life.

10. Carry on looking for all the other rubbish you want to buy.

11. Discover you have started making a strange 'bip' noise with your mouth every time you buy anything, as though you are running it over a barcode reader.

12. When you have finished shopping, select the 'Checkout' button.

13. Get your wrinkly partner to come and stand next to you for a few minutes, muttering words of admiration for all the different special offers and bargains that have come up on your list of items purchased.

14. Realize the price charged for delivery completely cancels out all the savings you've made on the special offers.

15. Pay for your items. No, they don't accept cash online.

16. Do a small lap of honour round your living room to celebrate having finally finished.

17. Look at the time.

18. Realize you could have gone to the shop and back in person in the time it's taken to work out how to use the website.

19. Wait for your shopping to arrive.

20. Realize you're feeling a bit peckish.

21. Decide to pop out to the shops to get something to eat to keep you going.

22. Arrive back home and discover a note through the door telling you that you have missed the delivery of your online shopping because you were out at the shops when it arrived.

Chapter 3:
Let's Get Comfy

Comfort is to the wrinkly as water is to the fish, as sunshine is to the flowers, and as daft comparisons are to analogies. In short: indispensable.

This is why wrinklies are so often reluctant to leave the comfort (note the important word there) of their own homes. The epicentre of the wrinkly's palace of pampering is the front room, and more specifically the wrinkly's very own armchair.

This simple piece of furniture is the crème de la crème of comfort. It is the ultimate in wrinkly wallowing.

With cushions carefully plumped, comestibles and beverages within easy reach and a cornucopia of diversions at hand, it has the power to evoke from the wrinkly a satisfied 'Aah, that's better...' when he or she lowers their tired old body into its welcoming contours and crevices that over the years have moulded themselves satisfyingly into mirror images of the wrinkly's own idiosyncratic contours and crevices: here a wrinkly hillock, there a soft furnishing valley, and so on.

The emitting of this wrinkly sigh of bliss when sitting down has led some to describe the armchair as 'furnitaah'.

The bed, of course, comes a close second in the furnitaah stakes, but it is not the haven of first resort after wrinkly exertion, and does not have the same feeling of being the hub of the wrinkly's universe.

At this point, some wrinklies will exclaim, 'But what

about the sofa, the settee (or, for posher wrinklies, the divan or the chaise-longue)? Me and the missus like nothing better than to get settled on the sofa of an evening.'

Yes, but sofas have to be shared. No sooner are you comfortably settled with a nice cup of tea and a piece of Victoria sponge than you are being asked to 'budge up'. This doesn't happen with armchairs. Therefore, for the purposes of this chapter, and indeed the entire book, the armchair has to be seen as the zenith of wrinkly comfort.

Once settled in the aahmmchair (*Stop it! – Ed.*), the self-pampered wrinkly must have everything within easy reach: The TV remote control, a variety of reading matter, perhaps a puzzle or two (they now have special jigsaw tables for armchair puzzlers), snacks, drinks, telephone… in fact, everything that one could possibly want.

Once happily settled, the wrinkly does not want any interruptions, so part of the comfort strategy is to minimize unwanted telephone calls, people ringing the doorbell and other flipping nuisances.

The wrinkly will also want to consider the optimum clothing for comfort, and the exact temperature to which the heating must be set. He or she must decide whether a household pet is an aid to comfort or a hindrance: foot-warmer or foot-nibbler?

It's not easy taking it easy. But this is your handy guide – to be kept by your armchair, of course.

The Wrinkly's Comfort Scale

The Beaufort Scale is used to measure wind conditions. At home in their armchairs, wrinklies use a similar empirical system:

Comfort Number	Description	Wrinkly's Condition
0	Extremely uncomfortable	Wrinkly rises vertically as a result of sitting on an upturned drawing pin.
1	Uncomfortable	Wrinkly drifts from chair to chair trying without success to get comfy.
2	Slightly uncomfortable	Gentle rustling heard from lumpy cushion beneath wrinkly's bottom.
3	Mustn't grumble	Cushions begin to move slightly as wrinkly attempts to get comfy.
4	OK	Noticeable breeze produced as wrinkly plumps his or her cushions.
5	That's better	Paper begins to move as wrinkly picks it up and settles down to read.
6	Getting comfy	Some joints heard cracking as wrinkly relaxes into chair.
7	Comfy	Wrinky sinks into cushions.
8	Quite comfy	Wrinkly engulfed with cushions.
9	Nice and comfy	Wrinkly now so comfy that getting up again will prove difficult.
10	Lovely and comfy	Roof tiles rattle with wrinkly's gasp of delight on sitting down.
11	Very comfortable now, thank you	Windows may break with the wind produced by wrinkly's exhalation of relaxation.
12	Ultimate comfort!	Whole buildings shudder as wrinkly moans loudly and writhes around in ecstasy at experiencing such comfort.

The Fine Art Of Cushion Plumping

It's a little-known fact that cushion-plumping is actually a martial art. Martial arts such as judo, sumo wrestling and karate are better known because of their fighting element.

It is probably quite true that Bruce Lee never made a film called *Enter The Cushion Plumper*, but somebody may have done.

Thought to have originated in around 4,000 BC, cushion-plumping probably didn't reach the West until the Norman invasion.

The timeline is thought to have been roughly as follows:

4,000 BC   In South-East Asia, an emperor known as Ez-charo complained that the horsehair-stuffed cushion in use on the royal throne was uncomfortable. He charged one of his courtiers with the task of sitting on the offending object for many hours before the royal posterior touched it in order to 'soften its barbarous bulk.'

1,500 BC   The practice of cushion-softening was taken up by the Babylonians, but with an ingenious twist; a Babylonian ruler by the name of Sofasrus realized that it was unnecessary for another bottom to touch the royal cushions, which by now were filled with goose feathers. He therefore invented a game whereby his soldiers would throw the cushion from one to another to soften it. This is thought to be how the modern game of rugby originated and is nothing to do with Rugby School.

200 BC   A Roman emperor, known as Comfus Maximus, further refined what we today would call cushion plumping by simply ordering one of his slaves to pummel the cushion mercilessly while imagining that it was one of his sworn enemies.

500 AD   The Roman occupation of what is modern-day
          France resulted in the French succumbing to
          what was considered at first to be the dastardly
          practice of 'le plump'. However, a French
          nobleman, Prince Louis Asseyezvous, made it
          fashionable in court circles.

1067 AD   Shortly after the Norman invasion, cushion-
          plumping was introduced to Britain. Britons
          were initially sceptical, partly because they first
          had to be introduced to furniture, but in time
          it became as much a part of British life as bear-
          baiting and public hangings.

So what can the modern-day wrinkly learn from our
past? What are the finer points of cushion-plumping?

1. Give yourself plenty of room. There's nothing worse
   than finding that, while your cushion is plumped to
   perfection, you have elbowed your wrinkly other half in
   the eye and caused mild concussion.
2. On no account over-plump. A common mistake for
   novice plumpers to make. Your beloved cush should not
   be reduced to mush.
3. Pick up the cushion and give it a quick shake.
4. Place the cushion on the armchair and pat several times
   with both palms.
5. Knead it with fists.
6. Give it a good flat-handed pummelling with both hands.
   It may help to imagine that you are either Keith Moon
   of The Who or Animal from The Muppets performing a
   wild drum solo.
7. Turn cushion over and repeat.

Other Things That Should Have Remote Controls

The TV remote control is one of the best things ever invented to keep the wrinkly in the comfort he or she knows to be one of their fundamental human rights.

The only wonder is that we don't have remote controls for other things too. True, you may have a remote control for your hi-fi system – a zapper for your Zappa, if you will – but what about your windows, your curtains: indeed, your wrinkly other half?

So, if there are any budding entrepreneurs or inventors out there, here is our wrinkly wish list:

- The kettle. As things stand, you have to wait until your wrinkly other half gets up to go to the loo and then casually and hopefully say, 'Putting the kettle on, are you?'

- The curtains. There you are; you've got as comfy as humanly possible, you've used the TV remote to put your favourite programme on, and then you can hardly see a thing because the sun has decided to come out and glare up the TV screen so all you can see is a reflection of yourself glowering at it.

- The windows. Knowing the vagaries of the British weather, it would be nice to be able to remotely open an inch of window when it suddenly becomes unexpectedly stifling hot in the middle of August.

- Furniture. Your telephone is handily within reach but then someone calls up and starts discussing some appointment or other which involves you getting up and finding your diary, pen and other paraphernalia before proceeding. If you could remotely summon your roll-top bureau to your side it would be a life-saving boon.

- The heating. The thermostat is inconveniently positioned just outside the kitchen on the wall of the hall. Fat lot of good that is when you are comfily cocooned in your armchair and need to nudge the heating a notch or two up or down.

- The front door. Or, more to the point, some sort of device that allows you to speak to callers from the comfort of your armchair. It is probably rather rude to tell unwanted visitors to 'Bugger off' without doing so face to face, but your comfort is paramount.

- Your slippers. Sometimes, your fervent desire to become recumbent as soon as you get back from the shops is so strong that you only realize after sitting down that you are still wearing your stout and sensible walking shoes. These, of course, are all very well for walking in, but they are not designed for leisurely comfort. Effectively being able to whistle your slippers in like loyal lapdogs would be footwear heaven.

- Your wrinkly other half. Yes, you can summon them in the customary manner, but wouldn't it be nice to be able to turn the volume down occasionally – or even completely off (much as you love 'em)?

What are the chances of any of this? In a word: remote.

Comfort Clothing For The Discerning Wrinkly

Trousers

An important part of being truly comfy is wearing the right clothing. You may already own a pair of 'comfort fit' jeans or casual slacks. 'Comfort fit' is marketing talk for 'Fit for people who either don't admit to their waist size or have no idea what it is.' But of course, that would be too long to fit on the label.

Closely related to comfort fit is 'expandable waist'. This makes a lot of sense because wrinklies themselves often have expandable waists. 'Another slice of Battenberg?' 'Oh, go on, then; I'll make room for it.'

And this is how you find your waist size inching up (or in some cases, footing up) from perhaps a 32 to a 36, then a 40, and finally, the expandable waist. After that there's nowhere to go and you can stop worrying about such trivial things and get on with the far more important task of enjoying yourself.

So, that's the trouser department sorted. Next: the top half.

Tops

Once upon a time the wrinkly's top half of choice was the cardy. It even sounds comfy, doesn't it?

The cardigan was named after the 7th Earl of Cardigan who fought at the Battle of Balaclava. Why anyone should go to war over items of winter woollies is a mystery, but we digress.

In these modern times, however, the familiar comfy cardy is being supplanted in some quarters by... the fleece.

This is all very well for youngsters and postmen, but wrinklies would have to try and get used to having a hulking great zip down the front of this garment. Wrinklies must make their own choices, but remember; modernity for modernity's sake is the enemy of comfiness.

Shoes

Or rather, lack of shoes. Shoes are to comfort what Usain Bolt is to a gentle stroll round the block. When re-entering the wrinkly residence it is customary, almost compulsory, to sit down, remove one's shoes, and say, 'Ah, that's better!'

Slippers are the order of the day when relaxing. Whether they're tartan, fluffy or bearing images of cartoon characters is a matter of choice, but again, the accent must be on comfort.

It's a fact of life that as we pass the first flush of youth our feet begin to remind us that they have walked the equivalent of the entire circumference of the Earth in their lifetime, and they're not going to let us forget it.

Chilblains, corns, bunions, swelling: the wrinkly foot is a micro-climate of medical misery quite separate from the rest of the body.

Accessories

Immediately following the arrival of your winter fuel bill you may take to wearing gloves, scarves and hats indoors to get the next bill down to double figures, but apart from that the list of comfort accessories is mercifully short: an old blanket (tartan, of course), to put over the knees, perhaps some footballer's socks (i.e. thick) and you're sorted.

The Pecking Order Between Wrinklies And Household Pets

Do you defer to your dog? Do you cosset your cat or suck up to your stick insect?

In other words, who rules the roost in your house – you or your pet?

Now, we all know that the British are a nation of animal-lovers, but surely there should be some limits. If you don't watch out you may soon come home to find your pampered pooch sitting in your armchair reading the paper and expecting you to go and rustle him up some grub while he just finishes the crossword. What do you mean, he already does?

All right; it's time to start setting some limits here: laying down a few laws. And if you've been letting your furry friends walk all over you they may not like the new regime.

So, just to get you started, we present on the following page a few pointers as to where you may be going wrong.

It's the wrinkly guide to the difference between good pet ownership and frankly barking pet ownership.

And if your pet is at the moment looking over your shoulder at this book, cover its eyes – it may not like it.

Good Pet-Owner	Barking Pet-Owner
Your dog has a little jacket for the cold weather.	Your dog has an entire walk-in wardrobe of designer clothes.
You keep a packet of crunchy treats for your cat.	Your cat is addicted to balsamic vinegar and sea salt crisps.
Your tropical fish have little arches to swim through.	Your tropical fish have a scale replica of the lost city of Atlantis to swim around in.
Your gerbil has a nice wooden cage with an exercise wheel.	Your gerbil has a nice wooden cage with a fully-working running machine.
Your budgie is allowed out of the cage to fly round the room occasionally.	Your budgie has been trained to take your letters of complaint to the local council offices.
Your pet snake is allowed out for an occasional slither.	Your pet snake is allowed to terrify visitors by slithering up their legs unexpectedly.
You teach your parrot to talk.	You get annoyed when your parrot refuses to discuss the current economic crisis with you.
You occasionally bring the rabbit in from his hutch to play.	You can't understand your rabbit's inability to grasp the simple rules of Monopoly.
Your pet mouse is rather partial to having his head stroked.	Your pet mouse expects nothing less than an entire body massage and pedicure.

The Fine Balance Between Warmth And Bankruptcy

What was that quote from Dickens? 'Annual income twenty pounds, annual expenditure nineteen and six, result: happiness. Annual income twenty pounds, annual expenditure twenty pounds and sixpence, result: misery.' This can be adapted for the wrinkly, especially the retired wrinkly, to: 'Weekly pension ninety-odd quid, result: misery. Weekly pension ninety-odd quid, weekly fuel bills ninety odd quid, result: not only misery but starvation too.'

Yes, feeding the wrinkly's fuel habit is an expensive business. Pound for pound, gas and electricity are more expensive than gold. OK, that's because gas and electricity don't actually weigh very much, but you get the point.

Heating a modest wrinkly house nowadays will cost a shivering arm and a goose-pimpled leg. So what's the answer? Wrinklies are nothing if not inventive and these are some of the ways they will manage to keep those bills down:

Going to the library

Why do you see so many wrinklies in the library? Is it because they're all extra-mature students? Is it because they scorn daytime TV and would rather curl up with a Tolstoy or two? Are they going there to improve their computer skills? No, they're trying to keep bloody warm.

Sitting in cafés

Never mind les rues de Montmartre; café society wrinkly-style is the greasy spoon down at the wrong end of the high street where you can still get a cup of tea for less than a quid. And while your heating is switched off at home you are effectively earning about 50p an hour in saved heating bills. Spin that cuppa out for a couple of hours and you're in profit. You're hired!

Visiting 'friends'

By 'friends', we mean anyone you happen to have bumped into over the entire course of your lifetime. The key phrase here is: 'I/we were just passing...' Not only will you save on fuel bills, you will also be quids in on tea, biscuits, cake and maybe lunch too.

Working in the charity shop

It's wonderful that so many people of a certain age (all right, wrinklies) give up their free time to help others. The fact that every unpaid day working in the shop is saving a small fortune in heating bills is just a happy bonus.

Extra layers

You may not want to go out. You may be expecting visitors, or there's something good on the box or, irony of ironies, you're waiting in for the gas man. Do you think that's why they're so notorious for keeping you waiting? No, of course not, but it makes you wonder, doesn't it?

So the thermostat goes down, and you go upstairs to pull out anything that might keep you warm – bobbly old jumpers, fingerless mittens so you can still pick up your jigsaw pieces, blankets, woolly hats – so that when the gas man finally deigns to turn up, he wonders whether you're about to enter a Sir Edmund Hillary lookalike competition.

How To Minimize Daily Distractions

We may have said this before, but we wrinklies are busy people. We lead busy lives. The demands on the everyday wrinkly are great; the responsibilities hang heavy. What we don't need, therefore, are interruptions. We have lawns to mow, letters of complaint to write and little DIY and decorating jobs to do around the house, the extent of which make the painting of the Forth Bridge look like a doddle. In short, we're up to our myopic eyes in it. The last thing we want is some buffoon knocking at the door and asking us if we want to buy dusters, double-glazing or eternal life.

So, here is a handy cut-out-and-keep guide to micro-managing those daily distractions:

Cold-calling telephone sales people

Let them spout their carefully-scripted bit of pseudo-polite waffle (they're paying for the call, after all), then equally politely ask them to hang on a moment. Continue with what you were doing before they rang. After an hour or two you will probably find they have hung up. With a bit of luck they'll blacklist you and never call again. Hooray!

Doorsteppers

They usually want to sell you something or ask you to contribute to a charity. One way or another, they want your dosh. The fact that you are a wrinkly and haven't two brass farthings to rub together is neither here nor there. The trick is to turn the tables: sell *them* something. 'Ah, I'm glad you've called. We've got this old sofa/clapped-out TV/set of curling tongs...' You won't see 'em for dust.

'Friends'

Have you noticed that the only people who ever call on you unexpectedly are the very ones you don't want to see? And there is also the possibility that they are fellow-wrinklies who, having read the previous section of this very book, are coming round for the sole purpose of keeping their own heating bills down.

This is where your curtain-twitching skills come in. Always keep the downstairs front curtains drawn; then sidle up to establish through the minuscule gap between curtain and window frame whether it is in fact Doris and Stan from number 47. If they are seasoned cold-callers, however, be ever-vigilant for them peeking back through that minuscule gap themselves, only to find you hunched guiltily against the wall and having to explain it when you reluctantly invite them in.

Your wrinkly partner (female)

If you are a male wrinkly you may find that no sooner are you happily settled in your armchair than your wrinkly other half trolls in with the J Edgar and commands you to lift your feet while she fusses around with the business end of the vacuum cleaner. This is where wrinkly ailments come into play. You can't possibly lift your feet because a) you've put your back out again, b) your rheumatism's giving you gyp, c) the old knee cartilage is playing up again.

Your wrinkly partner (male)

Would you Adam and Eve it? You've been going on at him since 1997 to fill that hole in the ceiling from his doomed attempts at fitting a tasteful chandelier in the front room, and now he's dragging the stepladder in just as your favourite daytime soap is starting. You therefore have to suggest that he goes to the pub for an hour. Of course, this may have been his strategy all along.

Dogs

Whoever said a dog is a man's best friend was talking twaddle. Would your best friend beg you to take them out for a walk in the pouring rain by making pathetic whimpering and howling noises? Would they foul the air of your living room and expect to be rewarded with a biscuit? Would they attempt to jump on your lap when you were asleep in the armchair? In a word, no. There's nothing else for it – swap him for a budgie.

Cats

Cats are a bit more subtle, but can still stand between you and armchair nirvana.

As soon as you're out of the room to fetch a cuppa they're up on the chair and fast asleep, trying to give the impression they've been there all day. They will not respond to flinger-clicking, pleas or even scary-voiced exhortations to shift. They have to be picked up, still in the foetal sleeping position, and deposited elsewhere.

Then you can't properly relax because you feel guilty. See? They always win in the end.

Chapter 4:
Everything Nice And Handy

We wrinklies like to have everything immediately to hand.

This is because ever since passing the age of 40, wrinklies have been making grunts and groans akin to those produced by a Wimbledon champion every time they have to get themselves up out of their armchairs.

When a wrinkly sits down again, he/she will invariably let out such an intense gasp of satisfaction that passers-by will wonder what on earth they're getting up to.

If, therefore, a wrinkly has to get up and sit down too often there is a good chance that he/she will either have a heart attack, put their back out or be arrested for indecent behaviour. Or, even worse, all three.

Wrinklies therefore have to keep movement from their armchairs to an absolute minimum, and ideally even less than that. This can be achieved by ensuring the chair is perfectly positioned and by having everything that is required within easy reach.

The wrinkly armchair must be placed so as to provide clear lines of sight to the television screen, the living-room window, the front door, the kitchen (to see when the emanation of a plume of steam from the kitchen door announces the kettle has boiled) and the cat flap (in case the wrinkly moggy gets stuck on the way in).

This luxuriously cushioned observation centre must also, of course, be adjacent to a heat source such as a gas fire, a radiator or one of those big blue sock-like devices that plugs in to warm up your feet.

A wrinkly's armchair must also have a veritable armoury of remote-control devices balanced on its armrests.

The wrinkly then sits like a Wild West sharpshooter

ready to whip out one of this vast array of remote controls and to aim and fire it at one of the electrical devices in the room. These may include a television, a DVD player, an ancient video recorder, a digital or satellite box, a radio and a CD player.

The number of electrical devices in the room will equal the number of remote controls minus one. One remote control will exist for a mysterious device that is no longer present and the nature of which cannot now be recalled.

Thus surrounded by communication devices, gadgets and reference materials, a wrinkly's armchair will end up resembling some sort of mission control – albeit one in which the mission in question is to get through as much daytime television and as many hot drinks as humanly possible.

A telephone, book, magazine rack, pen, paper and wallet or purse will also all lie within easy reach. For objects slightly out of arm's reach, wrinklies have mechanical grasping devices bought long ago from the Innovations catalogue. For picking up objects even further away than that, wrinklies have obedient and long-suffering spouses.

Eventually, a wrinkly may have everything so nice and handy that it will be possible for them to survive for several years without ever having to leave their armchair – apart, that is, from having to go to the toilet every half-hour.

The Ideal Wrinkly Armchair

So what special features might the world's ultimate armchair for wrinklies boast? How about:

Luxurious cushions, but not quite so luxurious that the wrinkly occupant of the chair will slowly be consumed by the cushions, eventually disappearing from view never to be seen again.

Kettle and tea things hidden in the armrests.

Options for reclining and swivelling, moveable head rest and elevating footrests. Basically, it must have every feature possible to help transfer responsibility for the movement of joints from the wrinkly's own body to the chair.

A lift in the seat to help the wrinkly get up out of the chair without completely exhausting themselves in the process. The lift should not however be so sudden and powerful that it will fire the wrinkly occupant out of the chair into the air and spring them through the living room window into the front garden.

Castors, so that the chair can be moved around without the wrinkly having to stand up. Ideally, it will be possible for the wrinkly to wheel themselves in their armchair all the way into the kitchen and back again.

Massage option in cushions to give the wrinkly a nice back rub and which can, in an emergency, be turned up high enough to restart his/her heart.

Headlights and indicators in armrests – just in case the castors run a bit too freely and the wrinkly ends up trundling away down the road outside while still sitting in their armchair.

How To Exercise Without Moving

Wrinklies need to do a bit of exercise now and again in order to try to counteract the general process of ongoing decay and degeneration (or ageing, as it is more popularly known).

There is, however, a dilemma for health-conscious wrinklies. Even if the wrinkly brain knows that exercise might be a good idea, the wrinkly body will undoubtedly think otherwise and will probably refuse to get out of the comfy armchair.

Even if the wrinkly brain manages to persuade the wrinkly body to attempt some physical exertion, a further problem exists. Wrinklies are all too well aware that any sudden movement will inevitably cause them to put their back, neck, knee and/or false teeth out.

Ironically, exercise will probably leave a wrinkly completely unable to move and the wrinkly body will tell the wrinkly brain, 'Now, why couldn't you have just listened to what I was telling you?'

It would therefore be helpful if wrinklies could exercise using as few sudden movements as possible. Ideally, the wrinkly should exercise without moving their body at all. But what are the options?

Canadian Air Force exercises

These exercises were developed in the 1950s and can be done in just 11 minutes a day. This leaves you 23 hours and 49 minutes to sit stuffing yourself with biscuits. The exercises involved are: stretching; sit-ups; back extensions; push-ups; and running on the spot. Four of these sound like things a wrinkly would do in his/her armchair anyway.

Exercise game consoles

Another brilliant idea. Now you can exercise by watching a pretend you running around on your TV screen. You can use systems such as the Wii console to play tennis or golf or to box, cycle or do aerobics.

You may wonder if the manufacturers of these devices are in fact taking the wii wii. Nevertheless, exercise using such consoles can apparently be almost as strenuous as the real thing. You can increase your heart rate and work up quite a bit of a sweat. And that's just from trying to get the thing out of the box, wired up and working properly.

Thinking about exercising

Ah! Now we're getting somewhere. Stories regularly pop up in the newspapers claiming that scientists have discovered it is possible to achieve almost as much benefit just by thinking about exercise as it is by actually doing it.

This is good news for wrinklies, who prefer to think about many things these days rather than actually doing them. Even better, you can think of yourself doing your exercises in the most exclusive gym you can imagine and save a fortune on membership fees at the same time.

On the other hand, while scientists may have shown that ordinary people can achieve a physical benefit just by thinking about exercise, have they repeated their tests on wrinklies? Might their results in fact suggest that wrinklies will be just as able to slip a disc when thinking about exercise as they are when physically jumping about the place?

Bits Of Their Bodies That Wrinklies Are Likely To Put Out If Things Aren't Left Nice And Handy

Backs

Wrinklies tend to put their backs out more often than they do their cats. If a wrinkly has to stretch two millimetres too far to pick up the TV remote control, they will sit back and discover that their vertebrae are no longer stacked in the usual order.

The wrinkly will then stagger around the house in some apparent discomfort with his/her arms outstretched. This will make him/her look not unlike Frankenstein's monster.

For this reason the best treatment may be to strap the pained wrinkly to a large slab in the attic and run a few million volts through their body in an attempt to jolt them back into shape.

Necks

A wrinkly can put his/her neck out just by saying 'No' too emphatically. This will leave the wrinkly with their head balanced on top of their shoulders at a bizarre angle, looking as though someone has pulled it off for a moment before shoving it back in a rather careless manner.

The wrinkly will then wander around with their eyes bulging in pain and with a fearful look on their face in case anything gives them the tiniest unexpected jolt. They will nevertheless keep imploring their wrinkly partner to get hold of their head by the ears, pull it and then let go abruptly, as though it will then magically spring back into position.

Shoulder

Stretching too far for the remote can leave a wrinkly in a permanent state of shrugging one of their shoulders but not the other.

Ankle

Basically, wrinklies can put out any joint anywhere in their body by doing anything – even if it doesn't involve the joint in question.

Hands

Wrinklies quite like it when bits of their hands get put out of joint because they can then spend a happy few minutes trying to click everything back into place. They will sit in their armchairs clicking and clunking away, apparently re-assembling the bone structure of their hands, as though their skeleton were made of Sticklebricks.

Knees

Another bit of the wrinkly body that seems to regularly pop out at random. This leaves the wrinkly sitting massaging their kneecap, apparently trying to move it around inside their leg and position it back where they think it should go. This bizarre form of amateur self-surgery seems to be based on the idea that wrinklies' bones can be moved around from place to place under the wrinkly skin. This would mean that every time a wrinkly stood up their bones would tumble out of place – which, as we have shown, is exactly what tends to happen.

Boomps-a-daisy

No wrinkly needs to be told just how painful it can be if you put out your boomps-a-daisy.

How Much Is The Stuff In Your Living Room Worth? The Wrinkly's Guide To Antiques

As you gaze round the room from the comfort of your armchair, you may begin to wonder how much all the items therein are worth.

In fact, you may even have a bit of an inkling. After all, you are an avid watcher of TV shows about antiques, attics, car boot sales, auctions and all the rest. You've probably been watching *Antiques Roadshow* since you were knee-high to a Chippendale cabinet.

So, let's tot it all up.

The old wooden bureau

This is clearly an antique. It had bow legs before you did. The lovely walnut finish, a bit like you after that fortnight in the Algarve, the little compartments for stamps and suchlike. OK, there's a splash of peach gloss down the back, but it's out of sight, and yes, one of the legs is a bit wonky, but all in all, surely it must be worth, ooh... £500?

The Blue Lady

Not all wrinklies appreciate art, especially if it's unmade beds and stuffed whales or whatever. But this – it's mysterious and enigmatic, like the Mona Lisa, but blue. Plus, it's irreplaceable because the shop you got it from, Woolworth's, is no more. £150?

The quirky chess set

Not everyone's cup of Darjeeling by any stretch, but how many people can honestly say they have a chess set where the white pieces are based on Snow White, with the pawns being dwarves, and the black pieces are all *Star Wars* characters, with Darth Vader as the king? No, it didn't cost a lot, but it can only increase in value with the passing years. £250ish?

The old radiogram

Many's the time you've thought, 'It's got to go.' When, you ask yourself, did I last tune in to Hilversum or the Home Service? Especially since your nephew bought you that digital radio for Christmas. But... it would be like parting with an old friend. £800, but it's not for sale.

The coffee table

Now, this definitely can go. In a moment of madness, sometime around 1973, you were persuaded that a Perspex coffee table was the thing to have. Tasteful brass fittings, magazine rack underneath, no sharp corners to bang your legs on; it was state-of-the-art. Now it's just a state. £20, no questions asked. All right, a fiver.

The armchair itself

This, my friend, you may well say, is not for sale. Some things are beyond price. It would be like Lewis Hamilton selling the driving seat from his first Formula One car – or something.

After this quick survey you conclude that, coffee table aside, you are probably sitting on a small fortune. Trouble is, you don't want to sell it. You therefore sit back, surveying your material wealth in the sure knowledge that if the worst came to the worst you'd be in clover with this little stash.

Handy Gadgets That Will Drive You Insane

It seemed like a good idea at the time: long-handled toenail clippers to save you bending down or adopting a yoga-style position before you could get on with the pedicure.

Apart from the fact that they look terrifyingly like a set of long-handled garden secateurs that could lacerate a limb without a by-your-leave, you had failed to take into account the fact that if your foot was not either two inches or eight feet away from your eyes you couldn't clearly see your toes anyway. Hah! So much for progress.

But over the years you seem to have accumulated a small armoury of useless items that, far from making your life easier, have actually made it more infuriating.

It probably all started with the Teasmade. If you needed a machine to make the tea for you, why did they invent marriage? It doesn't make any sense.

And with the advent of the microchip, boffins have been beavering away at new-fangled this and new-fangled that in order to make our lives easier. Well, perhaps they would do if you could ever lay your hands on the flipping things when you needed them.

In the meantime your house resembles the stock department for the Innovations catalogue.

So let's present here the myth and reality of 'useful' gadgets.

Myth	Reality
A handy device to transfer all your old vinyl records to CD.	You now have CD tracks that jump and make a sound like someone cooking up a full English breakfast.
The portable doorbell, handy for when you're gardening.	Every time someone calls at the front door, you can hear a faint, distant 'Ding dong' but can't quite place where it's coming from.
Slippers with torches on the front, handy for those midnight toilet excursions.	First, you still have to find your slippers in the dark, plus you can stub your toe just putting them on.
The timer clock on the cooker that will tell you when dinner is ready.	This only ever seems to go off when you're on the phone or on the toilet.
The TV remote control to save you getting out of your armchair to switch channels.	You spend ten minutes hunting for it under the sofa, down the back of the armchair...
The food mixer – handy for whizzing up winter soups.	The injuries you have sustained from trying to clean those razor-sharp blades have persuaded you to go back to canned soup.
The telephone answering machine to field those unwanted calls.	Hardly any bugger leaves a message, so you still have to get up during your favourite TV programme to dial 1471 because the suspense is just too much.

Why Do Things Disappear The Moment You Put Them Down?

Never mind the Bermuda Triangle; you have the equivalent in your very own front room.

Logically, it just doesn't add up. You have a relatively small confined space with a finite number of objects in it. Therefore, ipso facto and all that, nothing can be lost.

In reality, of course, it's very, very different.

You once saw a TV documentary about wormholes in space. This cosmic conundrum postulates that things can disappear from one part of the universe, whizz through a wormhole and then reappear somewhere else. You know the feeling: your glasses, for instance. You put them on the arm of the chair, get up to put the kettle on, come back, and they're gone. Disappeared. Even as you search down the back of the armchair they are hurtling through one of these wormholes, only to suddenly reappear somewhere quite unexpected – for instance, on the end of your nose.

You know you didn't leave them there. You would swear on oath that you didn't, but there they are.

Same with your keys. You are just about to leave the house and you check to make sure you've got your keys, and would you believe it, they've vanished. With your skills you could probably join the Magic Circle. Harry Houdini, eat your heart out.

And it doesn't stop there. Even within the tiny area occupied by you and your armchair, things will go walkies.

For instance, the TV remote control to which we alluded a couple of pages ago. How does it do that? How can it just... disappear?

It could explain a lot of things, your armchair. A quick feel down the sides will garner a wealth of bits and pieces, from rubber bands to hearing aids. Who knows, perhaps the Mary Rose is down there somewhere?

Then there are VERY IMPORTANT THINGS like tickets.

Clearly the safest place in any wrinkly household is behind the clock on the mantelpiece.

You would think that this area would be sacrosanct, beyond such fiendish physics as wormholes etc., but no. The moment you are about to set off to your concert, dinner dance, quiz night or whatever, the all-important tickets have disappeared. They were there this morning, you say. Ah, yes: but so was the sun and even that's disappeared now.

You then accuse your wrinkly other half of moving them, to which they respond by firing back with something you managed to lose just yesterday, and then, like some miraculous sleight of hand, they reappear – probably in your pocket. This, of course, is after you have double-triple- and quintuple-checked behind the damned clock.

Because you simply can't understand why something isn't still where you left it. People will josh you about 'senior moments', but you're having none of it.

It's clearly a cosmic conspiracy, akin to Sod's Law, and you finally have to admit that, like Sod's Law, there's not much you can do about it.

What's Down The Back Of A Wrinkly's Armchair?

Crumbs

A wrinkly's armchair will have, contained within its cushions, the remains of every meal and snack that a wrinkly has ever eaten while sitting in it. Clearly when wrinklies eat something sitting in an armchair they decide to share half of what they're eating. It's as though they believe their chair were some sort of living creature like a constantly hungry pet dog.

If the disgusting remains are ever exhumed, there will be enough to fill several baskets, as though in recreation of the biblical story of the feeding of the five thousand.

This presumably means that, over time, a wrinkly's armchair will grow bigger and bigger as the wrinkly fills it up with bread, cake and biscuit crumbs. If you are now having to use a stepladder to get up into your armchair, it may be time to buy a new one, or at least to stick the Hoover attachment down the back of the cushions.

Remote control

A TV remote control will also inevitably have found its way down into the bowels of the wrinkly's armchair at some point. The loss of the remote may have been treated as a mystery and a replacement device purchased: and yet, with a TV remote submerged deep underneath his/her buttocks, the wrinkly occupant of the armchair will now sit wondering why the TV keeps changing channel every time he/she shifts in his/her seat or breaks wind too forcibly.

Coins

The depths of a wrinkly's armchair will also be filled with coins. No-one ever suspected that the chair was a thief and yet for years it has been filching money from its occupant like some sort of upholstered pickpocket. Pulling out the cushion from a wrinkly's armchair will reveal a gleaming miser's horde. The chair's wrinkly occupant will then believe themselves rich, until they notice that the coins are all foreign or no longer legal tender.

Hair

Wrinkly men may wonder where their hair has gone. One look down the back of the armchair will surely reveal the answer. To the great frustration of the balding wrinkly, every coin, biscuit and peanut to emerge from between the cushions will appear more fully hirsute than himself.

All a balding wrinkly needs to do is to cover his shiny bald pate with adhesive and stick it between the armchair cushions once a week, and presto! A full head of hair once again!

On the other hand, this technique is also likely to result in balding wrinklies getting coins, biscuits and peanuts stuck to their heads.

Medicine

If wrinklies have to pay for their prescriptions, the discovery of a lost pill down the side of the chair cushions will prove just how high prescription charges are. Unlike all other foodstuffs, a pill will be deemed fit for consumption no matter how aged, hairy or furry it turns out to be.

Grapes

Even if the wrinkly resident of the armchair has never eaten a grape in their life, a hairy discarded grape will somehow have become lodged in its dark and clammy depths. Despite the number of years for which it must have been lost and the fact that its best-before date must have been some time in the previous millennium, the grape will still appear relatively plump and juicy and only slightly shrivelled. Clearly, stuffing grapes down inside armchairs and regularly squashing them beneath a warm pair of wrinkly buttocks is not an effective way of converting them into raisins and should therefore not be used by wrinklies as a means to set up a business enterprise supplying the public with dried fruit.

Peanuts

Strangely enough, peanuts smell like they have spent some time in the depths of a wrinkly's sofa even when the pack is freshly opened.

Winning lottery ticket

Damn! The wrinkly owner of the winning ticket will have turned the entire house upside-down trying to find this before finally slumping into his armchair in resignation. The armchair will then slyly reveal the missing ticket by letting it slip from its cushions at precisely midnight on the day it becomes irredeemable. The armchair does this out of sadistic cruelty towards the wrinkly who parks their buttocks on it every day. The armchair's wrinkly owner will then give themselves a heart attack trying to lift it up and throw it through the living room window in frustration.

Chapter 5:
What's On Telly, Then?

To many wrinklies, the TV is like an old friend: that is, a familiar object sitting in the corner repeating the same old stories you've heard dozens of times before. Plus, once in full flow it is strangely difficult to switch off. But, like an old friend, where would we be without it?

Over the years we've all been through periods where we say, 'Right; I'm going to cut down on my TV viewing. I'm going to read more books, take up a hobby, make an effort to go out, do some exercise, etc. etc. etc.'

Of course, in the cold light of day, all that stuff seems an enormous faff, and the following evening you're sharing your leisure time once again with your old mate Cathode Ray, despite your misgivings. These can be summarized as follows:

- There's nothing worth watching.
- It's all repeats.
- There's too much swearing, sex and nudity.
- The only thing you can find in the schedules that you want to watch this evening is on a channel you haven't got.
- Why can't they make programmes like they used to?
- Why don't they bring back *Play For Today*, *Bonanza*, *The Price Is Right*...?

You, no doubt, will have your own personal wish list/ hit list of how to improve TV, but essentially it all amounts to the same thing; if you were in charge, television viewing would once more be a delight and a highlight of your evening.

73

The great thing nowadays, though, is that you can be master or mistress of your own destiny, or even your own *Dynasty*.

Almost any TV series worth watching is available on DVD, video or even YouTube if you happen to have any truck with such new-fangled gadgets.

At the touch of a button you can watch *Hancock's Half Hour*, *The Forsyte Saga* or even Borg winning Wimbledon. The only danger is that, one evening while you are sitting watching an episode of *The Waltons* and find your mind wandering off to subjects such as what shade of magnolia to paint the skirting board, you realize that not every single episode was a classic after all.

You come to the slightly scary conclusion that even *I Love Lucy* and *Bilko* may have had their off nights. This leads you to think of what else you could be doing with your time of an evening.

The wrinkly is nothing if not resourceful and can turn his or her hand to anything from scale models of the Taj Mahal made out of ear-cleaning cotton sticks to a lounge Las Vegas using Custard Creams as gambling chips.

When all else fails, there is the wrinkly imagination. To infinity and beyond!

Yes, with a lifetime of reading, experience and the odd bit of daydreaming, the outer limits of the wrinkly universe are boundless.

TV? Who needs it?

Armchair Theatre

Once upon a time there was a very good series of plays on TV called *Armchair Theatre*, which featured new writers such as Alun Owen and Harold Pinter. Whatever happened to them? Sadly, the series finished in 1974 and there's been very little worth watching on the box ever since. However, you can have your very own armchair theatre in the comfort of your own home without even turning on the TV. This could comprise one of the following:

Your spouse attempting to change a lightbulb

This three-acter features:

Act One:	Trying to find the bloody stepladder.
Act Two:	Trying to find a bloody spare bulb.
Act Three:	Wobbling on the stepladder and performing a Tarzan-like swing from the light flex (warning: this scene may contain strong language).

The dog chasing its own tail

Occasionally a dog will turn around for no apparent reason and be astonished to find a tail wagging somewhere in the region of its own backside. This, naturally, is alarming, so the dog will then attempt to hunt and catch this impostor. If you don't have a dog, you can simply watch a TV clips show where someone has sent in a video of this very same phenomenon.

Neighbours

Not the Aussie soap, but your very own neighbours who have inadvertently left their curtains open just prior to an almighty slanging match, possibly involving crockery. Enjoy!

Armchair Gambling And Other Ways To Avoid Dreadful Daytime TV

Via press reports, you will be aware that bookmakers these days are prepared to offer odds on almost anything: the name of the Beckhams' next baby, alien visitations, election results... in fact, the last two may not be entirely unconnected.

But why should bookies have all the fun? You too can lay a book on whatever takes your fancy, and within sight of the wrinkly armchair is a wealth of things you can gamble on.

So, invite your wrinkly friends round, attach your green eye-shield and place your bets, please.

- How many minutes will pass before some unwanted piece of junk mail flaps through your letterbox? Rest assured, you and your wrinkly friends will not have to pass many minutes crouched in the hall waiting for this momentous event. Odds of it happening in first five minutes: evens; odds of it happening in the first hour: 100 to 1 on; odds of the offending article being a pizza leaflet or a minicab card: 3 to 1 on

- The next utterance of your wrinkly partner. Odds as follows:
  Have you seen my glasses? 5 to 1.
  Are you putting the kettle on? 3 to 1.
  Isn't it about time you...? evens.

- Next caller at front door. Odds as follows:
  Jehovah's Witness/Mormon/Other religious person: 3 to 1.
  Salesman: 2 to 1.
  Neighbour coming to ask a favour: 5 to 1.
  Parcel for you: 50 to 1.
  Parcel for next door: 2 to 1.

- Identity of next telephone caller. Odds as follows:

  Salesman: evens.

  Wrong number: 2 to 1.

  Family member wanting to borrow money or ask a
  favour: 3 to 1.

  Friend phoning for a chat: 10 to 1.

  Secret admirer unable to contain their desire for you a
  moment longer: 1,000,000 to 1.

- An electronic household gadget giving up the ghost. You
  will have noticed that these things only happen at the
  very worst times, so odds are as follows:

  Cooker breaking down: 100 to 1.

  Cooker breaking down at Christmas: 10 to 1.

  Fridge conking out: 50 to 1.

  Fridge conking out during drought: 5 to 1.

  Video/DVD packing up: 100 to 1.

  Video/DVD packing up just as you are setting it
  before holiday: 3 to 1.

- Post (1) This is all about what time your post will
  actually arrive. Odds as follows:

  While you're still in bed: 1,000,000 to 1 (this will only
  happen if the postman got lost on yesterday's round
  and has turned up 16 hours late).

  Before lunch: 100,000 to 1.

  After lunch: evens (but almost certainly when you're
  out, if there's something to sign for).

- Post (2) This is about what you will receive. Odds as
  follows:

  Bill(s): 50 to 1 on.

  Junk mail: ditto.

  Someone else's mail: evens.

  A postcard from someone who's somewhere nicer and
  warmer than you: 5 to 1.

  A proper letter from someone you actually know: 100
  to 1.

  A large cheque: 14,000,000 to 1.

The Wrinkly's Wealth Of Armchair Literature

Imagine the British Library, the Bodleian Library and the Library of Congress all rolled into one, and it would be nothing like the average wrinkly's armchair library. That's because the wrinkly's armchair library isn't just books, schmooks; it's a wealth of written material, the variety of which is truly mind-boggling to the average non-wrinkly.

So, what does it consist of?

Books

Yes, there are books of course: lighter books for inducing sleep and heavier books for balancing up the wonky coffee table.

Newspapers

The newspaper is a versatile object. When the sun streams in and you're too tired to get up and close the curtains it makes a handy sunshade. When you fancy 40 winks during the hours of daylight it is like an aeroplane sleep mask. It is an oversized coaster for putting your tea mug on to avoid leaving rings on the coffee table. It is an effective fly-swatter; it is handy for mopping up spillages; it can be used to start a real fire in your grate; it provides hours of origami-based diversion. At Christmas it can be turned into a cheap party hat. It can be rolled into balls and dangled on string for the amusement of your cat. In extremis, it can even be read.

Magazines

For particularly persistent or heavily-built flies, this is the nuclear option in the arsenal of the insect-irritated wrinkly. But beware; the satisfying thwack it makes as you jubilantly whack it down could in fact be the sound of your lovely teak coffee table being rent asunder.

Medicine instructions

How they fit them into those tiny boxes is anyone's guess, but as you unfold those microscopically printed leaflets out again and again you suddenly find you have almost enough to wallpaper your entire living room. In our experience the last page is usually the most entertaining/frightening. This will list all the things the medicine might do to you. We use the word 'might' advisedly, because to cover their backsides the medicine manufacturers will list everything from mild vomiting (have you ever heard of anyone vomiting mildly? No, neither have we) to spontaneous human combustion.

Bumf

As you probably know, this is short for 'bum fodder', though how many people do you know who actually feed their own bottoms?

This consists of leaflets that drop out of your newspaper, junk mail that has found its way to your inner sanctum and, other assorted rubbish that you might idly read because the newspaper is just out of arm's reach.

Guarantees/insurance policies, etc.

These are the things you never look at until something goes wrong. You then dig them out of the shoebox only to discover that:

a) The faulty item is out of warranty/not covered by insurance.
b) The sub-clauses and exclusions mean you haven't got a leg to stand on.

The Wireless – TV For The Ears

Yes, the wireless: not the radio, thank you very much. The wireless is Wogan, Ken Bruce, *Desert Island Discs* and the shipping forecast; the radio is thump, thump, thump all day long and an endless stream of prattle from some semi-literate buffoon who probably doesn't even wear a tie when he's broadcasting.

No, in our opinion it all went downhill when they shut down the pirate radio stations. Note that they never called them pirate wireless stations, did they?

Up till then we had the Light Programme with *Workers' Playtime* and *Two-Way Family Favourites*, the NDO and the afternoon play.

If you wanted to listen to incessant pop music you could tune into one of the pirate ships and hear Napoleon XIV and 'They're Coming To Take Me Away, Ha Ha' and endless jingles about how wonderful the radio station was.

Even the pirate stations in those days still played a nice tune occasionally, but if you wanted proper wireless entertainment it was the BBC (not the Beeb, thank you very much).

Then they decided to shut down the pirates and hire all their seasick DJs to work for Radio 1, which is rather like the Admiralty catching lots of real pirates and putting them in charge of the Royal Navy.

So the Light Programme was no more. This is probably when the Sunday roast bit the dust too.

It's almost certainly nigh-on impossible to cook a leg of lamb and stewed cabbage properly if you're not listening to *Life With the Lyons* or *The Billy Cotton Band Show* at the time. When they swapped *The Clitheroe Kid* for Kid Jensen the writing was on the wall.

Educating Archie, *The Goon Show*, *The Brains Trust*, *Hancock*… all gone, and the world's a poorer place. Because the wireless was TV for the ears.

And this is where the wrinkly imagination comes in.

When we listened to *Dick Barton – Special Agent* we could see him in his trilby and mackintosh defying death rays, catching kidnappers and foiling foul plots.

Thanks to the wireless, the wrinkly mindscape is filled with hurled batter puddings, elephants called Nellie and, most mind-bending of all, a radio ventriloquist. Any fool can look at a ventriloquist on TV and see whether his lips are moving, but to deduce that from listening to him on the wireless takes a real leap of imagination.

So when modern-day wrinklies sit down and listen to the wireless they will be forming pictures in their minds, painting landscapes, murals, backdrops and sets filled with characters.

Non-wrinklies will have the radio on in the background while doing something else, little realizing what they're missing.

Perhaps the answer is to find an old radio with a proper light-up dial where you'll see the magic words 'Light Programme' or 'Home Service', and perhaps, just perhaps, you might be able to tune in to a crackly old episode of *The Navy Lark*.

Wakey wakey, wakey wakeeeeeey!

The Winding-Up Of Cold-Callers

Most people see cold-callers as a nuisance. Wrinklies should see them as a source of endless entertainment.

All it takes is a bit of preparation. Whether it's someone calling on the telephone or at your front door, you will be the Jeremy Beadle to their poor unsuspecting punter.

The Hard Of Hearing

Telephone caller: Hello, is that Mr/Mrs Smith?
You: Hello?
Caller: Is that Mr/Mrs Smith?
You: Hello?
Caller: Is that Mr/Mrs Smith?
You: Half-past four.

At this point the caller should hang up, but remember, they've got other calls to make, and you can keep this up all day.

The Confused Old Person

Telephone caller: Hello; is that Mr/Mrs Arbuthnot?
You: Did you hear that whistling noise?
Caller: Hello? What whistling noise?
You: Listen... hear it?
Caller: No.
You: They're tapping my phone.
Caller: Who is?
You: Marks & Spencer. Ever since I took that pullover back...
Caller: Click.

The Contrary Customer

Telephone caller: Have you thought about changing your electricity supplier?
You: Yes. I'm glad you called.
Caller: (Surprised) Are you? OK, can I take a few details?
You: OK.

You then proceed to give them all the details they want, real
  or imagined.
Caller: Fine; so if I can just take your bank details?
You: Actually, you know what? I think I'll just stick with
  the lot I'm with. Better the devil you know and all that...

The Ultra-Keen Buyer

Doorstep caller: Hello; have you ever thought about double-
  glazing?
You: Thought about it? I've dreamed about it.
Caller: Oh, good. Right; I'll just run you through a few
  options...
You: Can you do it today?
Caller: What: fit the windows?
You: Yes.
Caller: Well, not exactly today, but...
You: Sorry; it's today or nothing.
Caller: Er...
You: 'bye then.

The Listener

Doorstep caller: Hello; I'd like to share the good news with
  you.
You: Mm-hm.
Caller: I expect you've often wondered what life is all about...
You: Mm.
Caller: Now, I've got a few pamphlets here that you might
  be interested in...
You: OK.

They can deal with arguments – they have counter-
arguments – but it's very hard to argue with someone who's
agreeing with everything you say. They will eventually
wander off, slightly dazed, in the hope of having a good old
argument next door.

The Wrinkly Puzzle Page

Odd One Out

Spot the odd one out in the following lists:

- a) Smiling, happy, vivacious, fun-loving, wrinkly.
- b) Young, thrusting, fashionable, gorgeous, wrinkly.
- c) Tolerance, fair-mindedness, patience, understanding, wrinkliness.

Complete the Phrase

- a) He who laughs last…
- b) If you pay peanuts you get…
- c) It takes two to…

Who Said The Following?

- a) We will fight them on the beaches.
- b) Never! Never! Never!
- c) Lend me your ears.

Answers

Odd One Out

- a) Happy – he's one of the Seven Dwarves.
- b) Young – he was in a band with Crosby, Stills and Nash.
- c) Patience – it's a card game.

Complete The Phrase

- a) …is getting a bit hard of hearing.
- b) …wrinklies.
- c) …get a decent state pension.

Who Said The Following?

- a) Wrinklies attempting to get sun loungers before Germans.
- b) Wrinkly refusing to buy on hire-purchase scheme.
- c) Wrinkly attempting to hear at the theatre.

Chapter 6:
Who The Hell's This Now?
The Wrinkly's Guide To
Visitors

Oh, no! Here they come! Just when you've got comfy in your armchair! Still, it's nice to have visitors, isn't it?

OK. Calm down. There's no need to start swearing like that.

Visitors provide wrinklies with news, with company, with a receptacle in which to dispose of cakes that have recently passed their use-by date and with an exercise in lateral thinking (when it becomes necessary to dream up imaginative yet polite ways to encourage them to leave after they have outstayed their welcome).

Wrinklies can expect to receive two distinct sorts of visitors. There are perfect visitors and there are the sorts of visitors wrinklies get in reality.

Wrinklies' visitors turn up apparently under the assumption that the wrinkly's home is some sort of drop-in centre offering a range of services.

Firstly, the visitor will regard the wrinkly's house as a lovely, cosy café in which all the food and drink on the menu is served free of charge and where there is no need to tip the catering staff.

Secondly, the visitor will see the wrinkly's house as some sort of medical centre where they can unburden themselves of the details of all the most intimate, terrible and/or contagious ailments that are currently afflicting them.

And thirdly, the wrinkly's home will be regarded by the visitor as a place in urgent need of interior design advice which only they will be qualified to provide.

A time of arrival will have been agreed by both visitor and wrinkly visitee. The visitor will invariably be the one who fails to arrive at the agreed time. By contrast, the wrinkly visitee will be at the appointed meeting place at the agreed time without fail – because they live there.

The wrinkly visitee nevertheless has a reason to agree a set time of arrival with their visitor. This is because the agreed time provides them with an idea of when they should make a final trip to the toilet before their visitor turns up.

Certain visitors will, however, attempt to thwart this plan by turning up a few minutes early in order to catch the wrinkly still in the toilet.

The visitor's repeated chimes on the wrinkly's doorbell will then elicit a tinny response of 'With you in a minute' echoing from the bathroom tiles. The visitor will then make their grand entrance to the sound of the gushing fanfare created by the toilet recently being flushed.

Even worse than this are visitors who turn up late. The kettle has to be kept in a state of permanent near-boiling in expectation, while the wrinkly sits anxiously as though awaiting the visit of a member of royalty or the arrival of the likes of Eric Clapton live on stage.

Yes, there are only two problems with a wrinkly's visitors. One is the time they arrive and the other is the fact that they arrive at all.

Welcome and Not-So-Welcome Visitors

Welcome Visitor	Not-So-Welcome Visitor
Arrives carrying a large bag filled with cakes and goodies.	Departs carrying a large bag filled with cakes and goodies (the bag having been empty when they arrived).
Tells you all the latest stories they have heard of local gossip, scandal and acute social embarrassment.	Tells you all the latest local gossip stories only for both of you to realize halfway through that they are all about you.
Listens to all your problems.	Leaves you with a lot of extra problems.
Congratulates you on all the home improvement work you have had done.	Leaves you feeling you need to get lots of home improvement work done.
Tells you that you have made their cup of tea just the way they like it.	Gives you a lengthy impromptu training course on how to make a cup of tea just the way they like it.
Brings you lots of stories about your neighbours.	Leaves to share lots of stories about you with your neighbours.
Greets you with a hug and a little gift.	Greets you with a hug and a little gift of seasonal flu.
Listens to all your news in confidence.	Reports everything you say to the local news bulletin.
Doesn't outstay their welcome.	Is still sitting on your sofa when you go up to bed that night.
Listens to everything you have to say.	Switches on your TV and tells you to 'shut up' because they're trying to watch something.

Things You Are Likely To Be Doing The Moment An Unexpected Visitor Turns Up At The Door

Sitting on the toilet

Unexpected visitors like nothing better than catching you when you are in the toilet. Presumably they hide and use binoculars to keep a beady eye on your bathroom window until they know you're in there. Once the door's locked and you're fully engaged, as it were, these rascals race to your front door and ring the bell.

What can you do? You can't pretend you weren't in the toilet by leaving it unflushed, because your guest will undoubtedly check on the situation when they go to use your facilities.

No, there's nothing for it; the noise of the toilet flushing will be echoing throughout your home as you open the door to greet your guest, who will be left with the not unreasonable belief that when left alone in your house, you spend your entire time sitting on the toilet until someone arrives.

Settling down to watch a favourite TV show

Of course, it won't be a worthwhile programme like a scientific or historical documentary. No; it'll be some sort of guilty pleasure, your addiction to which you would prefer to remain unknown to friends and associates. And so the first note of the *Neighbours* theme tune will immediately be followed by the doorbell ringing.

Climbing into a nice hot bath

What are you going to tell your visitor? 'Come on in! Get your kit off and join me!'

Making a cup of tea

Visitors must sit a little way down your road in some form of covert surveillance van filled with equipment tuned to detect your kettle being switched on.

Making yourself a nice cup of tea will cause visitors to mysteriously appear as though from nowhere. Naturally, they won't appear the moment you switch your kettle on. No; they will wait until you are just settling down with your drink. You will then have to get up again to make one for them. Then when you both sit down your visitor will have a steaming fresh mug of tea, while your own drink will have cooled to a barely warm coagulating brown residue.

Laying out your underwear on the radiators to dry

You have just washed all your wrinkly old underwear (not a single item of which has been purchased since the turn of the millennium).

You have almost finished laying out every piece of this historically interesting range of undergarments so they are now displayed on every radiator in every room in the house.

The doorbell rings just as you place your final holey, yellowy pair of pants on the last available centimetre of radiator space. You then have to sprint back round the house in silent-movie-style fast motion, speed-collecting all your pants back into the laundry basket. You can then hide them in a kitchen cupboard where they will remain out of sight until your visitor discovers them half an hour later while searching for the biscuits.

Etiquette When Entertaining Guests: Some Do's and Don'ts

Do: greet your guest with the words: 'How lovely to see you!'

Don't: greet your guest with the words: 'Bloody hell! What d'you want this time?'

Do: welcome your guest into your house.

Don't: charge them an admission fee.

Do: take your guest's hat and coat and put them in the cloakroom.

Don't: take your guest's hat and coat and put them on eBay.

Do: show your guest into the living room.

Don't: show your guest into the downstairs toilet, telling them, 'Sorry; I was just in the middle of something when you arrived.'

Do: immediately place the small gift your guest has brought you somewhere it can be seen and admired.

Don't: immediately place the small gift your guest has brought you in a charity collection bag by the front door.

Do: ask your guest exactly how they would like their tea or coffee.

Don't: then thrust a mug in their hands and say, 'Tough luck!'

Do: allow your guest to choose from a range of delicious cakes.

Don't: allow your guest to watch as you consume a range of delicious cakes.

Do: engage in a range of conversational topics with your guest.

Don't: sit doing animal impressions every time your guest tries to say anything.

Celebrity Visitors And Why They Probably Wouldn't Suit Wrinklies

HM The Queen	Having Her Majesty round for afternoon tea might impress the neighbours, but what if she decided to start turning up on a regular basis? The cost of installing a brand-new toilet seat ready for each visit would surely be ruinous.
The Prime Minister and his Cabinet	Politicians look so young these days, they would probably all ask for glasses of squash rather than a nice cup of tea – then they'd get hyperactive, go a bit mad with the economy and it would be your fault for filling them with E numbers.
The Rolling Stones	Whatever they normally have with a cup of tea you've probably not got in your kitchen cupboard.
The Archbishop of Canterbury	Your tea would probably go cold while he was saying something wise about your Mr Kipling Almond Slices.
David and Victoria Beckham	He'd leave muddy footprints all over your carpet if he forgot to wipe his boots but, on the plus side, she doesn't look like she'd get through too many of your French Fancies.
Pete Doherty	You couldn't trust what he'd get up to while you popped out to pour the tea. It wouldn't look good if photographs appeared in the press of him taking drugs while standing in your front room between your rubber plant and the framed photo of your niece getting married.

Types Of Visitor To The Wrinkly Home

News at Ten:

Spends their visit sitting on your sofa telling you story after story relating to neighbours, friends, friends of friends, etc., whether you want to hear them or not. They may even end by giving you a brief weather forecast for the neighbourhood just before they leave.

The Medical Specimen:

Comes to entertain you with all the latest news on their fascinating range of medical conditions and current medication. How they made it to your house without the aid of an ambulance is a mystery.

The Thinker:

Sits in silent contemplation for the duration of their visit while you drive yourself crazy trying to get a conversation going.

The Hooded Figure of Death:

Sits on your sofa grimly pronouncing the latest in an ongoing list of your friends, acquaintances, etc. to have passed on.

The President of Your Fan Club:

Spends their visit expending extraordinary amounts of enthusiasm in their admiration of every tiny aspect of your home or detail of your life.

The Air Freshener:

Their fragrance (or odour) will mysteriously remain in the air throughout your house for hours or even days following their visit.

The Food Taster:

The true purpose of their dropping in on you quickly becomes apparent.

Suitable Topics Of Conversation (And Some Less Suitable Ones As Well)

Suitable: a polite enquiry into your guest's current state of health.

Less suitable: a polite enquiry into whether, given their appearance, your guest has made their funeral arrangements.

Suitable: a discussion of recent weather patterns.

Less suitable: a discussion of recent weather patterns with reference to the evident damage that these have caused to your guest's hair.

Suitable: an enquiry into the current activities of members of your guest's family.

Less suitable: an enquiry into the current criminal convictions of members of your guest's family.

Suitable: a nice bit of juicy gossip.

Less suitable: presentation of a slideshow showing clear photographic evidence of your guest's spouse's infidelity.

Suitable: asking your guest's views on cosmetic surgery.

Less suitable: offering to arrange cosmetic surgery for your guest.

Suitable: asking if your guest has read any good books recently.

Less suitable: asking if your guest is able to read.

Suitable: the latest dietary advice.

Less suitable: trying to sell your guest your used gastric band.

Suitable: a final enquiry into when your guest intends to visit again.

Less suitable: an enquiry into when your guest intends to visit again so you can arrange to be out.

The Wrinkly's Guide To Door-To-Door Salesmen

Satellite TV

A succession of greasy-haired, spotty-faced young men in suits will turn up at your door and look astounded when they learn that you don't wish to pay £50 a month for several hundred extra channels broadcasting rubbish to add to the hundred free channels broadcasting rubbish you currently receive. Well, it already takes you all day every day just to scroll through all the channels you currently get before declaring, 'There's nothing on!' and going back to bed.

Gas and electricity

Another series of helpful young men will appear at your door to tell you just how much you could be saving on your gas and electricity. These incredible savings can, however, only be demonstrated by means of advanced mathematics. They will then pour scorn and derision on you if you do not immediately wish to hand over your bank details to start receiving your energy from South Uist Nuclear Fission Ltd. Another way to save on your energy bills would be to slam the door on them and keep the heat in.

Double-glazing

Every window in your house is already double-glazed, you have a double-glazed conservatory and a double-glazed porch, and your bifocals are probably double-glazed as well. Nevertheless, double-glazing salesmen will knock on your double-glazed front door, stand watching you approach through the double-glazed panel and then greet you with the words, 'Hello; have you ever considered getting double-glazing?'

Dusters

Dusters and various other cleaning products that you never run out of are regularly brought to your door by slightly disturbing-looking individuals. The dusters offered will be priced at a level several thousand per cent higher than similar products available in local shops. Nevertheless, pointing this fact out in a loud voice will probably result in unhappy consequences. possibly involving a demonstration of light dusting being performed on the floor of your hallway using your face.

Religious people

Be careful. You might end up living the next few decades of your life as part of a cult just because you were too polite to tell them to bugger off.

Tree surgeons

Speculative visits from these door-to-door lumberjacks seem to occur more frequently than might be expected.

Strange foreign women selling bizarre dolls

Very occasionally you will discover a couple of women in unusual ethnic garb standing on your doorstep. They have come, it seems, from some far-flung place where life is hard and wages are preposterously low. This would obviously be a situation with which you would feel some pity, were it not for the fact that these women have decided to adjust the economic imbalance between their country and yours single-handedly. After a few minutes' awkward conversation in a mixture of languages, you will find that you have agreed to purchase a small doll for which you have no use whatsoever for the same price as a two-week luxury holiday in its country of origin.

Ways To Pretend That You're Not In

Wow; there must be some people whom you really don't want dropping in to visit you. If so, try some of the following techniques to avoid being detected at home:

- Close all the curtains and blinds, switch off the TV and lights; it will then be very difficult for people to see if you're at home. Unfortunately you will be left trying to move round your house in total darkness. Passers-by may therefore be alerted to the fact that someone is at home by the bangs, crashes and shouts of agony emanating from your house.

- Try and remain absolutely quiet so people can't tell that there's anyone in the house. This technique will not, however, work on its own. Passers-by will not think there is no-one at home if they can see you and your wrinkly partner acting like a pair of Marcel Marceau-style mime artistes in the middle of your front room.

- Do not answer your phone. If you answer your phone by mistake, pretend to be your answering machine and end anything you say with the word 'beep'. Callers will not be convinced if you answer your phone and then try telling them, 'Hello. No, this isn't me. I'm not at home at the moment.' They will also not be convinced if you pretend to be your answering machine but then offer to put your wrinkly spouse on the line.

- Don't take in your newspapers or milk bottles. However, don't neglect to do so for so long that your neighbours get worried and call the emergency services. Your front door will then be smashed in by concerned-looking paramedics to whom you will have to explain that you were just trying to avoid a visit from a dull friend who always eats all your cakes.

- Move about your house out of sight by crawling around underneath your carpets at all times. This is obviously quite difficult and physically demanding, plus you may end up with carpet burns on the top of your head.

- Try camouflage. You and your wrinkly partner can daub each other in make-up the same colour as your three-piece suite and wallpaper. The pair of you can then sit and watch telly in the front room without being spotted through the window, although some eagle-eyed passers-by may wonder why your three-piece suite suddenly looks a bit worn and wrinkly.

- Arrange to have thick metal shutters fitted to all your doors and windows. Don't arrange to have this done while you're hiding inside, though, in case it leaves you not only unable to be seen or heard but also unable ever to get out again.

- Set fire to your house. This usually deters most visitors, with the exception of the fire brigade. On the plus side, they don't usually stop for a cup of tea during one of their visits.

Things To Say To Your Guests When You Want To Try And Encourage Them To Leave

Have something else to eat; I've got loads more stuff I need to get rid of because it's been in the cupboard so long.

Don't worry; I'm probably not very contagious any more.

It's just coming up to the time of day when I like to sing a few hymns. Shall I get you a song sheet?

Did I ever show you the photos I took during my hernia operation?

I know; let's play a game.

I made these scones to help take my mind off my skin condition.

If you'd like yet another cup of tea, please don't worry; I can always pop out to the shops to get some more milk, sugar and tea... again.

So even after hearing about my conviction, you were still brave enough to call round.

Oooh! I think I can smell the smell that the dog makes when it's time for his suppository.

It's just coming up to what I like to call 'naturism time'.

Surprisingly enough, the last eight people who sat where you're sitting have all died, but that's probably just coincidence.

I'm sorry, could you just remind me – who are you again?

Chapter 7:
Nodding Off

There's something rather delicious about dropping off in the armchair: something slightly decadent. One minute you're sitting upright and the next you're slouched back, head tilted to one side, eyes closed and mouth open. This is slightly embarrassing if you're hosting a meeting of your book club at the time.

Isn't it slightly odd, too, that while a wrinkly can take hours to get off to the land of Nod in the piece of furniture upstairs specifically designed for sleep, he or she will be snoozing like a baby without even trying within moments of settling in the armchair?

There must be a psychological element to it. Somebody should write a book about it: *The Psychology of Psnoozing*, or something. When you want something to happen it steadfastly refuses to, and when you don't want something to happen – bingo.

Story of your life, really, isn't it? Ours too; tell us about it.

Plus, of course, snoozing is entirely different from sleeping. Sleeping is a biological necessity; snoozing is... well, a guilty pleasure, really.

In theory, you're supposed to be sitting down writing the shopping list or phoning the gas man about the boiler or making an appointment at the vet's, or something. But somehow, the sheer effort of picking up pen and paper has worn you out. So you lean back for a couple of minutes and... suddenly there are more Zs than a Polish telephone directory.

Then there's the strategic snooze. Yes, we've all done it, haven't we? The other half wants to go out for 'a nice walk' or whatever and we, quite frankly, can't be fagged, so with the aid of a few exaggerated snores we manage to get out of it.

Elementary wrinkly tactics, really: but what happens when you drop off at a very important moment, such as the start of your favourite TV programme or when you've arranged a rare snifter or two with friends in the pub? Disaster!

Or at least it would be, were it not for wrinkly ingenuity. Before settling in the armchair, just set one of those timer thingies to turn on the toaster, which is pre-loaded with bread and set at its highest setting. When the very, very, very well done toast pops up, the resulting fumes will set off the smoke alarm and have you up and about in no time.

But what is it exactly that makes your eyelids droop in the first place? Daytime TV, obviously. The scintillating outcome of whether someone sells their antique chamber pot for £3 or £3.50 at auction is hardly worth staying awake for, is it?

Then there are the guests. Fascinating though Mr Thompson from next door's verrucas may be, an extended health bulletin would severely test the alertness of a hopeless insomniac, not forgetting the sheer exhaustion induced just being a wrinkly for yet another day – phew! Let's just have 40 winks...

Sleeponyms

We all like a little sleep in the day but we don't like to admit as much, so we have invented lots of other ways of referring to it. Which, of course, is fooling no-one, but it makes us feel better.

These are just some of the phrases crafty wrinklies will use:

Getting my head down for five minutes.

Resting my eyes.

Catching 40 winks.

Resting at anchor.

Just putting my feet up.

Having a bit of shut-eye.

Enjoying a siesta.

Meditating.

Taking a breather.

Taking five.

Meeting the sandman.

Crushing the cushion.

Testing out the sofa.

Examining the backs of my eyelids.

How To Avoid Offending Your Guests

A cynic would say that the best way of avoiding offending your guests would be not to not invite them round in the first place, because as sure as eggs is eggs there will come a point when they suddenly seem slightly less fascinating than they did when they walked in. Their conversation will suddenly take on the gentle, lilting tones of a stage hypnotist willing you to sleeeeeep. The combination of soft furnishings and hot sweet tea (or something stronger) will soon have you nodding nicely.

There are several tactics available, though, to avoid being crossed off someone's Christmas card list.

Flattery

When you suddenly jerk awake to find your guests looking askance at you, simply say, 'What you just said has really made me think. I had to mull it over for a few minutes before I could answer.' With a bit of luck they'll gloss over the fact that you were dribbling and snoring while you were mulling.

Blind them with science

Tell them a recent study has shown that interesting conversation can actually increase alpha waves, which has the contradictory effect of inducing sleep. Thus, the more fascinating their conversation, the greater chance of you catching a few Zs. Beware, though, that if they're taken in by this they may stay and rabbit on for hours.

Blind them with history

Tell them that in ancient cultures such as the Mayan civilization it was considered the height of good manners to drop off mid-conversation. In fact, there was no greater compliment to your guests than to drown out their conversation with loud snoring.

Pretend you were acting

When you stir from a dream only to find a room full of people staring at you, jump up and say, 'How was that? Was that convincing?' Explain that you have just joined the local amateur dramatic society, have landed the part of Rip Van Winkle and have been demonstrating the role for their amusement.

Trendsetting

Issue all guests with travel cushions, blankets and other paraphernalia on their arrival and explain that they are allowed to have a little sleep whenever they fancy. Convince them that this is a new trend in fashionable circles and that it's common practice in the houses of Madonna, Stephen Fry and Lady Gaga. Your own nodding off will then be seen as the height of sophistication.

Dream analysis

When you wake up, tell your guests that you have just had the most amazing dream – starring them! As you weave the fantastic story of them winning the lottery, buying an island, living in luxury, inventing cures for all known diseases, becoming President of the world, etc. they will become so fascinated by their own fabulous story that they will forget it all started with you catching flies while they rambled on. Remember, though, to withhold vital little bits of information so they keep having to ask, 'And then what happened?'

Strategic Snoozing

Boring guests

Although sleep is a passive act, it can also be used very effectively as a weapon of war.

You've probably had guests who can't take a hint. As they go into intricate detail about their latest operations, the fabulous achievements of their children and grandchildren, or their exotic holiday plans, you stifle a yawn. When this doesn't work, you embark on a gargantuan yawn that makes the Grand Canyon look like a crack in the pavement.

If this fails there's the pointed look at the clock and a 'My goodness; is that the time?' This is followed up by the more desperate tactics such as winding the alarm clock, the donning of pyjamas etc.

By this time all but the most thick-skinned of guests will have taken the hint, but if all else fails then just pretend to go to sleep. Even the most case-hardened bore won't continue talking to someone who is clearly asleep. Be careful, though, to wait until you hear the click of the front door closing before you get up.

There's nothing worse than having your guest popping their head back round the door and saying 'Oh you *are* awake. I thought for a moment there you'd dropped off. Now, where was I...?'

Salesmen

If you've been daft enough to invite a salesman indoors the strategic snooze can be very effective in getting rid of him, though it tends to backfire if he's selling pep pills.

It may be that you don't even need to act asleep. After the third or fourth hour of a salesman explaining the fabulous advantages of double-glazing you will probably find that your eyes have (double) glazed over and that you are sleeping like a baby. The extraordinary thing is that when you awake you will find the salesman still prattling on and demonstrating the awe-inspiring functions of his unique windows: they open; they close!

It may take more than strategic snoozing to get rid of some of these people. Strategic clog-popping, perhaps?

Family

Families are like hot water bottles: all very nice for half an hour or so, but then the warmth wears off and you think about kicking them out.

It's bad enough when it's your side of the family but when it's your other half's lot, the strain of being polite for hours on end begins to take its toll: plus when you're a wrinkly the younger relations start to turn up with babies and small children over which you're meant to coo indulgently, even when they're wrecking your perfectly ordered wrinkly house and screaming the place down.

The well-timed yawn, the studied lid-droop, the rubbing of tired old eyes all come into play as the bairns rampage around the house.

The parents of these offspring will be so mightily impressed that you are actually managing to snore through what sounds like World War Three that they will gather up their brood and depart.

Daytime Alarms

Alarm clocks were designed to wake you up in the morning after several hours' beauty sleep. They weren't intended to rouse you after a crafty '40 winks' in the armchair.

Because the truth is that you never actually know when you're going to be having a quick nap. It just happens. Then you wake up to find your favourite daytime soap or game show is halfway through and you're cursing yourself for allowing such a thing to happen.

What you need is a daytime alarm. These can take the following forms:

Dog-owner alarms

When relaxing in the armchair, always leave a biscuit on your lap.

Well-trained dogs know that they are not meant to help themselves to treats and won't do it while you're awake. But when they see you nod off, doggy instinct will take over as they see their opportunity and they jump up to snaffle the tempting treat. You will then jerk awake just in time for *Deal Or No Deal*.

The Nodder alarm

This is similar to the above, but this time you balance something on your head – perhaps a plate or some other heavyish object such as a biscuit tin. While you are still in the land of the living the object will sit happily and harmlessly on your head, but as soon as that head begins to drop onto your chest the object will crash down into your lap and have you up and about in no time.

The water-feature alarm

Certain wrinklies like nothing better than to soak their feet – especially after some mild pedestrian exertion such as walking to the convenience store and back – so to adapt this simply:

1) Put feet into bowl of warm, blood-temperature water.
2) Soak feet happily.
3) In the event that you nod off the water will rapidly cool and wake you in a short space of time, perhaps with a sudden impression that you have lost all feeling in your toes.

The 'Noddy' alarm

Not to be confused with the Nodder alarm. This takes a little bit of preparation but is very effective and invaluable if you don't want to miss seeing the fate of the latest 'octochamp' on *Countdown*, for example.

1) Wear a hat with a little bell on it, rather like that of Enid Blyton's character Noddy.
2) Attach one end of some fine cotton to your eyelashes and the other end to the bell.
3) As your eyelids close the cotton will be pulled downwards, thereby ringing the bell on the hat.

The elastic alarm

1) Wrap an elastic band round each ear.
2) Lightly stretch the bands and wrap them around those little buttons that often feature in upholstery.
3) This will be comfortable when your head is leaning back but when it nods forwards the bands will stretch, detach themselves from the upholstery and thwack you in the back of the head.

Dreams Of The Everyday Wrinkly

There may or may not have been scientific studies into it, but somehow the dreams you have during the day seem rather different from those you have at night.

We've all seen those Freudian interpretations of night-time dreams; for example, when you dream of flying it either signifies freedom or tripping over the stair carpet.

Similarly, if you have a night dream about drowning it may mean either that you are being overwhelmed with problems or that your wrinkly other half has spilt their cocoa over you.

But when you sleep in the day your dreams are more likely to relate to events that are actually happening around you. For example, there is a clock ticking loudly on the mantelpiece. Your sleeping wrinkly brain will interpret this as a huge infestation of giant death watch beetles overrunning your front room. You will then leap from your armchair and smash the clock to smithereens before it eats your sideboard.

Or you hear the flutter of junk mail coming through the letterbox. Your overactive sleeping brain will interpret this as a Hitchcock-like visitation of crazed and ravenous meat-eating birds that are squeezing themselves through your letterbox to peck your eyes out.

When you awake to discover merely a leaflet offering 'Pepi's home cleening (sic) service's' you feel quite glad to see it for once.

Yes, the daytime events and noises going on within earshot as you slumber will translate into some quite terrifying dreams, as follows:

Humdrum Event	Wrinkly Dream
Your wrinkly other half is doing some hoovering in the hall.	You have inadvertently wandered on to a Formula One racing track and are all that stands between Jensen Button and a new world record.
The window cleaner is cleaning your windows with a squeaky chamois leather.	You are reliving the shower scene from *Psycho*, complete with screeching violins.
The dog is licking your face.	You are being seduced by someone with extremely bad breath.
Someone is ringing the doorbell.	You have gone back to work as an Avon lady – which is rather worrying if you're a wrinkly man.
The cat has jumped up and is purring loudly in your ear.	Your dentist is looming over you menacingly with a large road drill.
Your wrinkly other half has turned on the garden sprinkler.	The hissing sound is emanating from a large puff adder darting its venomous tongue at you and filling you with an urgent and inexplicable desire to rush to the loo.
You are snoring loudly.	You are a wrinkly caveman about to be devoured by a snarling tyrannosaurus.

Setting Endurance Tests

It's a long old stretch between breakfast and cocoa, and if you're going to spend virtually the entire time ensconced in the womb-like comfort of your beloved armchair then you're going to need some methods to keep you awake: coping mechanisms, they probably call them these days. You see? After all these years of watching daytime TV we're starting to pick up the jargon of all these lifestyle gurus, chat show hosts and the rest of the barmy army.

Perhaps it's best to start in small stages and work up. So perhaps the initial target should be staying awake for half an hour, then bump it up to an hour and so on until, before long, you're staying awake all morning. So, first off, how about this:

The party manifesto

Go to your local library and borrow a copy of one of the party political manifestos. It doesn't matter which one; they're all equally dull. After five minutes of 'goals', 'fairness', 'challenges' and all the rest you will feel your eyelids begin to droop. It's a wonder that Paul McKenna doesn't use the manifestos to lead people into a state of hypnosis. Muggers could use them to put people into a sleep state while they nick their wallets. You should be able to get them on prescription to cure insomnia.

So, once those eyelids begin to droop, force yourself to stay awake. If you can manage ten minutes on the first attempt you can stay awake through anything.

OK, you've passed the first test with flying colours; now on to the next one.

Legal documents

You thought the political manifesto was boring? Wait till you see this. Dig out some legal document from your last house move: perhaps some conveyancing thingy. After trying to extract any meaning from the first line, you may already be in the Land of Nod before you reach the first full stop. Haven't these people heard of punctuation? 'Whereas... blah, blah, blah, hereinafter... blah, blah, blah, aforesaid... hereby... whereof... yawwwwwn.....'

However tempting a bit of shut-eye may be, persist. If you can get through this and stay awake you're a marvel. Remember that some poor so-and-sos have to read this rubbish every day of the week.

Now for the big one. It's a shame that *Big Brother*'s no longer on TV, as that was probably the most boring programme in the history of television. So, failing that, this is probably the next best thing.

Parliament on TV

Short clips on the six o'clock news can be entertaining. A witty riposte here, a bit of banter there – perhaps even some mace-wielding if Michael Heseltine's around. But this stuff is on for hours every day and if detailed discussions of farming subsidies are not enough to get you off then the pretend-polite exchanges are: 'On a point of order Mr Speaker...' 'I am grateful to the honourable gentleman for his point of order.'

It makes watching paint dry look like a spectator sport.

Things Most Likely To Make Your Eyelids Droop

Where do we start? OK, we admit that some of this is down to personal preference, but here goes:

Televised motor racing

The cars go round the track: then they go round again, and again, and again, and again. Despite your humanitarian instincts you find yourself willing one of them to crash to liven things up a bit.

Televised golf

Another shot of the sky – how enthralling.

Televised cricket

That cricket's idea of a snappy, exciting game means only taking one whole day instead of three or four tells you something about the levels of endurance required to sit through this.

Television/film awards ceremonies

'I'd just like to thank my agent and my fellow-cast members and my director and my wardrobe mistress, and my mom and my dad, and my therapist, and...'

Radio phone-ins

''Allo Dave; I'm a cab driver, right, and I'm not a racist, but...'

And we haven't even mentioned other people's holiday photos, Twitter messages, detailed descriptions of other people's dreams, party political broadcasts, confessional TV programmes...

Chapter 8:
The Art Of Curtain-Twitching

It's important to look out for your neighbours. They may
have fallen ill and require assistance. They might need help
repairing damage to their property. They may have suffered
some misfortune and need someone to talk to.

Hopefully none of those things will happen to any of
your neighbours, but if they do you'll know which of their
do-gooding friends is first in line at their door because you'll
be craftily watching the whole drama unfold through a
small gap in your curtains.

Yes, secretly keeping tabs on comings and goings in the
street is a great wrinkly art. It's the main reason wrinklies
have curtains.

Curtains are not to keep the heat in, and certainly not
for visual appeal. No; if you see a row of wrinkly homes all
with the curtains drawn, there will be a wrinkly standing
behind each one, covertly surveying the scene like a Cold
War-era secret agent.

This explains why curtains traditionally come in pairs.
One side of the curtains accommodates a nosy wrinkly
husband, the other half his nosy wrinkly wife.

During the daytime the ultimate wrinkly invention comes
into its own: the net curtain.

The net curtain is a curtain designed to be left drawn
during the day so that no-one can see into a wrinkly's
house. This is because if they did, the first thing they would
notice would be a little wrinkly man or woman standing in
the window looking back out at them.

And what's the matter with that? The art of curtain-
twitching helps keep wrinklies' communication skills active.
If a wrinkly isn't sure why the man at number 24 is paying

so many visits to the woman at number 32, he/she and a few friends can sit round and spend several hours discussing the possibilities like a group of TV sports pundits.

Curtain-twitching can also help wrinklies forge new friendships – particularly with those down the road who possess more direct vantage-points into the windows of number 32.

And curtain twitching keeps wrinklies agile. This is because wrinklies who secretly observe someone in the street may have to make a sudden leap backwards if they believe they might be spotted. Some wrinklies are capable of performing a reverse high jump as they leap backwards over the top of the sofa away from the window, simultaneously closing the curtains as they do so.

Others, attempting to avoid being spotted at the window, have even perfected the reverse hop, skip and jump to take them not only over the sofa but then, in rapid succession, over the coffee table and cat as well.

Yes, it's just taking a healthy interest in the movements, feeding and mating patterns of the creatures seen outside your house. It's a bit like observing wildlife from a hide.

That's why wrinklies will spend the day behind their curtains with a sandwich, a thermos of tea and perhaps a pair of binoculars or night vision goggles.

I Wrinkly-Spy: Things You May Spot From Your Window

Award yourself the following Wrinkly-Spy points for spotting these things:

5 Wrinkly-Spy Points	20 Wrinkly-Spy Points	100 Wrinkly-Spy Points
Two women from up the road exchanging a cup of sugar.	Two women from up the road having an exchange of views.	Two women from up the road having an exchange of husbands.
The woman across the road putting her bins out in the road.	The woman across the road putting her husband's clothes out in the road.	The woman across the road putting her husband out in the road (preferably via an upstairs window).
Two of your neighbours talking over the back garden fence.	Two of your neighbours fighting in the back garden.	One of your neighbours in his back garden burying a mysterious object shaped a bit like one of your other neighbours.
The couple next door putting out their wheelie bin.	The couple next door arguing over whose turn it is to put the bins out.	The woman next door putting her husband out in the wheelie bin.
The police raiding number 52 and bringing out cannabis plants.	The police raiding number 52 and bringing out a suspect device.	The police raiding number 52 and bringing out Lord Lucan riding Shergar.

Everything You Ever Wanted To Know About Your Neighbours

'Neighbours,' as a wise man once said, 'Everybody needs good neighbours.' Unfortunately it seems that these days the good neighbours are all somewhere in Australia, running round next to a swimming pool and squirting each other with water pistols.

Since the dawn of mankind, people have lived in social groups and thus had neighbours. Having neighbours helps to share the essential functions required to maintain social life. The main examples of such functions must therefore be signing for your parcels when you're out at the shops and looking after your cat while you're away on holiday.

Neighbourhoods are defined as being local social units larger than households. A household, on the other hand, is defined as being the group that has to hush so they can all hear what the neighbours next door are arguing about.

People are believed to have lived in social groupings with neighbours for perhaps 100,000 years, this being the length of time that one family is known to have been waiting to get their lawnmower back from the people living next door.

Historical evidence for the existence of the world's first neighbours was provided by fragments of a 100,000-year-old cup found next to a wall in Mesopotamia. Obviously cups were first developed as devices for listening through the wall to what the neighbours were shouting about next door. It was several centuries before people realized you could drink out of them as well.

Some historians believe this advance may even have predated man's first learning to walk erect and stand on two legs. Historians believe that this development also derives from the existence of neighbours, as it must have occurred as a result of early humans having to stand up to be able to talk to the people next door over the garden fence.

116

Other important developments in ancient technology that derive from the existence of neighbours include the window, the curtains, the hedge and the Neighbourhood Watch scheme.

These days neighbours tend to be very annoying people. This is because they are always peeping out of their windows to see what you are up to. This is intrusive, impolite and something they have no right to do. As everyone knows, it should be YOU peeping out of YOUR window to see what THEY are up to.

The best neighbours to have are, of course, wrinkly neighbours. Usually wrinkly neighbours will have nice, quiet houses because they have at last managed to rid themselves of their noisy offspring.

Wrinkly neighbours may also be retired and will thus keep the neighbourhood looking nice because they can devote their every waking hour to keeping the exteriors of their homes in good repair.

Wrinklies are able to do this because they are always experts on the best paints and varnishes to help preserve crumbling façades, this expertise having been acquired during a lifetime's research trying to find the best products to apply to their own faces.

The Awesome Power Of The Wrinkly Imagination

Sitting in an armchair, it would not take long for the average non-wrinkly to be itching to turn on the box or possibly the Xbox or some other electronic device in order to entertain themselves.

The wrinkly, however, is a different beast from a different generation. We are old-school, and we know how to make our own entertainment.

This may be partly to do with the fact that in our younger days we had fewer than 60 TV channels to choose from and that even the couple of channels that were on finished with the epilogue at about half-past cocoa time. There was very little daytime TV (hooray!) and certainly no breakfast TV. In some households there may not have even been any breakfast.

Yes, we had it tough. How did we manage without iPods, iPads, mobile phones, DVDs, videos, the internet and all the other stuff?

We used our imaginations. And the wrinkly imagination is an awesome thing. Where a non-wrinkly might see someone delivering pizza leaflets across the road, the wrinkly will see a potential burglar casing the joint and have their finger poised over the '9' button on the telephone before you can say 'thin-crust Hawaiian with extra pepperoni topping'.

The wrinkly knows that the house at number 47 is a drugs den because he/she saw a swarthy-looking man emerge looking bleary-eyed at some unearthly hour the other morning.

The following table illustrates how differently the wrinkly mind and the non-wrinkly mind will interpret things.

Non-Wrinkly Observation	Wrinkly Interpretation
A milkman is delivering milk.	He is a KGB spy – even the letters on his float stand for Communist Observation Operational Person.
The dustmen are collecting rubbish.	Council snoopers are gathering information on your reading, eating and other habits for their secret files.
A man is cleaning an upstairs window.	He is clearly a Peeping Tom and needs to have his rungs severed.
A coffin is being taken from a house and being put into the back of a hearse.	This is obviously a very clever way of getting someone out of the house without being observed – probably a terrorist.
The woman at number 22 has put out two empty milk bottles when she normally only puts out one.	Either she has a fancy man or she is enticing the neighbours' cat away to save buying one.
There are men on the roof opposite slinging tiles into a skip.	Clearly a bunch of escaped convicts whose old habits die hard. Ring 999 immediately.
The new lodger at number 58 is going off early to work.	A strange man is creeping out of Mrs Peabody's at the crack of dawn hoping nobody sees him – well, I have!
The council men are unblocking the drain outside.	Plain-clothed police are dredging the drain looking for a dead body, most probably murdered in cold blood and dismembered in a particularly gruesome fashion.

Wrinkly Techniques For Peeping Through The Curtains

The secret agent

A pair of wrinkly eyes peeps through the middle of a pair of curtains, as though waiting for a coded signal from a secret informer somewhere outside in the street. Some wrinklies may go further than this and purposely cut eye-holes out of the middle of their curtains to ease their clandestine surveillance of the scene outside and to make it appear to passers-by that they have curtains with a strange bloodshot eye pattern printed on them.

The security guard

The imprint of a wrinkly figure can be seen slowly moving across each set of curtains in each room of the wrinkly's house one after the other.

The sharpshooter

The wrinkly stands at the centre of their living-room window with their back to the closed curtains. For a split second he/she peeps through the gap in the middle of the curtains and scans the view of the street outside before quickly hiding again.

Grandma's footsteps

The wrinkly peers through the curtains, spying on someone in the street outside, but ducks back in when the person turns in their direction. Unfortunately wrinklies are often not agile enough to get their heads back through the curtains in a hurry. The person outside in the street will thus turn and see a sight akin to a tortoise slowly trying to retract its head into its shell.

The headless spectre

The wrinkly shamelessly sticks their head through the middle of their pair of curtains to see what is going on outside. To outside observers it appears that a dismembered wrinkly head is floating in mid-air in the middle of the closed curtains.

Morecambe and Wise

This technique occurs when wrinklies who want to look outside and see what's happening have difficulty finding the middle bit of their pair of curtains. Outside observers will see the curtains rippling and thrashing around until a pair of wrinkly curtain-twitchers clumsily tumble into view, grinning sheepishly as they do so.

Behold my domain

The most shameless technique possible. The wrinkly stands in the middle of their front window with their curtains wide open, clearly not giving a damn who sees them surveying the scene. For added visual impact the wrinkly may stand in this pose with their hands planted firmly on their hips. A cape billowing behind them may complete the scene, making them look a bit like a superhero crimefighter ready to spring through the window at any moment and deal with any nefarious activity spotted in the tree-lined avenue outside.

The confused wrinkly

The confused wrinkly stands peeping through the middle of the curtains. Unfortunately he/she is standing on the wrong side of the curtains and is thus peeping back into his/her own living-room.

Looking On The Bright Side Of The World's Worst Neighbours

Everyone wants to live in a nice, quiet neighbourhood. On the other hand, there are few who don't enjoy watching their neighbours getting up to no good.

So lots of us seem to enjoy having neighbours who are badly behaved, as long as a) they perform their bad behaviour quietly between the hours of 10am and 8pm and b) the object of their bad behaviour is someone else.

Drug farm

Some wrinklies may discover that the house next door has been converted into a drug farm and is being used to cultivate illegal plants. But look on the bright side; many wrinklies have expressed the desire to live in the country. Now they can tell their friends that they live next door to a working farm. On the downside, the massive amount of electricity being used will cause next door's entire house to glow. The heat given off may, however, help to keep wrinklies warm in winter and if next door catches fire the fumes produced may be oddly relaxing.

Crack house

If the house next door is run-down and full of grey, awful-looking people lying around all day with a strange glazed look in their eyes, it's either another house full of retired wrinklies for neighbours or it's a crack house. If so, look on the bright side; the crack house's poor state of repair will make your own property look better by contrast.

Mafia headquarters

Potentially dangerous to have next door if you get into an argument with them about pruning their side of the hedge. On the other hand they are usually very well dressed, they will quickly and efficiently sort out any anti-social behaviour in the neighbourhood and they will probably be able to provide you with some excellent recipes for spaghetti sauce. Not only that, but they'll also offer you 'mates' rates' if you need them to sort out any problems with the other neighbours on your behalf.

House of ill repute

Imagine having a house of ill repute next door to you. It would be disgusting and appalling. Not only that, but you'd probably be kept up all night by the noise of the cash register going, whips constantly cracking in the bedrooms and people wandering up and downstairs while dressed in squeaky rubber wear. On the other hand, just think of the amount you could make in bribes if you happened to spot someone of note arriving there one evening.

Sweatshop

In terms of human suffering, it would be terrible. Nevertheless, you might still want to check if they have a factory shop selling their goods at even lower prices.

Dangerous dog-owner

The postman will probably be too frightened to deliver to them, so you could get your pick of anything they receive by mail order.

Student accommodation

No. Sorry. Can't think of any plus points on this one.

Tips On Dealing With Anti-Social Behaviour

Do: call the police if you spot genuinely criminal behaviour.

Don't: call the police out if you spot someone dropping a toffee wrapper.

Do: be careful not to provoke any groups gathering outside your house.

Don't: stand in your bedroom window giving them a lecture on the benefits of National Service through a loud-hailer.

Do: politely remind the offenders that their behaviour may distress any elderly people living in your street.

Don't: give the offenders the address of any elderly people on your street so they can go and distress them more directly.

Do: try to keep a discreet record of any misbehaviour you notice in case you need to report it to the police.

Don't: stride out into the street to try and catch the action on your cine camera while your spouse holds up an arc-light.

Do: phone up your neighbour so you can go out and confront the offenders together.

Don't: phone up your neighbour and then watch as he goes out to confront the offenders alone, wondering where you've got to.

Do: try engaging any miscreants in a non-confrontational manner, if possible.

Don't: come hurtling out of your front door towards them dressed in a Batman costume you once bought for a fancy-dress party.

Do: try and see which direction the offenders have come from.

Don't: try following them home and holding a tea dance in the road outside their house in an attempt to annoy them.

You Know You've Been Standing At The Window A Bit Too Long When...

- Your partner has started laying a place mat and dinner things for you on the windowsill.

- As they pass by your neighbours habitually turn and give a friendly wave towards the lumpy shape they can see behind your curtains.

- You don't feel properly dressed if you don't have a pair of curtains hanging over you.

- The pattern of your net curtains has imprinted itself on your face because you have been leaning against them too long.

- You can provide a detailed account of the movements of everyone in the street over the past year, even though you don't know any of them to talk to.

- When your partner isn't sure where you are in the house, the first place they check is behind the curtains.

- Your partner is happy for you to stay at the window all day because they've started regarding you as a draught-excluder.

- Even when you're not at the window there appears to be an imprint of your entire body left on the glass.

- You look up your house on the computer using Google Earth, only to see your own little face looking back out at you.

- Your skin is very pale apart from a single thin, vertical, tanned stripe running up your face where the sun has shone on you through the curtains.

The Wrinkly's Guide To People Working In The Street

Binmen

They ride into your street looking mean and moody, a bit like the Magnificent Seven but smelling of soggy cardboard. Leave your mess out for them but do not mess with them. They have the ultimate power over you. If you displease them they can leave a trail of your rubbish leading straight from your garden gate for all your neighbours to see: not only that, but they have access to a large mechanical crusher and they know the contents of your bin. That's not a Christmas tip you give them every year; it's hush money.

Recycling men

The environmentally friendly tribe who have evolved from your binmen and with whom they now alternate their visits. Their progress down the street is always entertaining. You can watch to see which of your neighbours is going to receive a notice telling them they haven't done their recycling properly this week. Those who persistently fail to wash out their baked bean tins properly may be punished by being brought out, strapped to the front of the recycling lorry and paraded through the streets like a discarded teddy bear.

Telephone men

They will dig an enormous hole in the road, spend the best part of a week sifting through masses of differently coloured wires and then at half past five on Friday evening they will accidentally snip through a single strand, leaving your whole street without telephone access for the weekend.

Gas and electricity repair men

Another group who like nothing better than to dig a big hole in the pavement and then spend the next few weeks sitting round it drinking tea and occasionally peering into it, wondering like the rest of us if a Doctor Who-style monster is going to come slithering up from the bowels of the earth at any moment.

Gas repair men are entertaining to watch to see which of them will be first to light a cigarette and blast themselves through next door's conservatory.

Electricity men are entertaining to watch to see which of them will tread on the wrong spot, crackle, turn blue and shoot over the rooftop like a firework.

Litter-pickers

Like sparrows, you used to see them all the time but now they seem to have become an endangered species. These days they are most often seen whizzing up and down your road in a small pod-like device that seems to be made from a lunar module welded together with a Dyson vacuum cleaner. In this vehicle they will pass through your neighbourhood like obsessively tidy aliens, hoovering up leaves, sweet wrappers, cats and any wrinklies who are a bit too slow crossing the road in front of them.

Surveyors

Rare visitors, but occasionally seen with large, pole-like devices and funny little things on tripods that look like toy cameras. They seem to be measuring the entire area just in case any local miscreants have stolen any of the road since they last measured it.

Qualities Required For Wrinklies' Curtain Material

Thickness – so it falls back into place very rapidly if you need to step away from the window in a hurry in order to avoid being seen.

Softness – in case you stand peering out of the window for so long that you fall asleep. The curtain material will then be soft enough to break your fall and keep you comfy during the night.

Blackout lining – otherwise the silhouette of a wrinkly body will be projected through the curtains for all to see.

High TOG rating – well, you might be standing there most of the night if something really interesting seems to be going on in the street.

Wipe-clean – if you're in there for a while you'll be eating and drinking.

Special printed design – if you don't have blackout curtains another option is to have curtain material made with a special design showing a group of life-size wrinkly people printed across it. Then passers-by won't notice you standing peering out of your window because you will just blend into the crowd.

Armholes – you've seen those blankets with armholes you can put over yourself to save on heating while you sit on the sofa all day. Surely the same firm must offer a similar line in curtain material for nosy wrinklies who want to spend the day peeping out of the front window but occasionally need to put their arms through to hold a hot drink or a biscuit?

Chapter 9:
A Nice Cup Of Tea And
A Snack

The armchair may be the centre of the wrinkly's daytime universe, but it would not be complete without a nice cup of tea and a little something to go with it.

But what is a 'nice cup of tea'? How does it differ from a mere 'cup of tea'?

Well, for starters, the best cups of tea are always made by someone else. When you're invited into someone's house you will invariably be greeted with the question: 'Would you like a cup of tea?'

This is what makes us British. Can you imagine a Zulu warrior inviting someone into his hut, popping on the kettle and producing a packet of HobNobs? Or a Frenchman? Or even an American?

But we digress.

At home, the best cup of tea, a 'nice cup of tea', is the one brought to you by your wrinkly partner unexpectedly. If it has a butter shortbread or two or a nice slice of Battenberg on the side, even better.

You can't properly wallow without a cup of tea and a snack. Hippos and pigs wallow in mud; we wrinklies wallow in armchairs and require the requisite refreshments to complete the fully satisfying wallow.

Aaah... that's better!

The armchair without a nice cup of tea and a snack is like a sauna without steam, like a gin and tonic without ice, like an analogy with nothing to compare something to.

So far, no-one has managed to establish exactly when the tradition of a nice cup of tea and a snack started, but there are rumours that this is why we lost the Battle of Hastings.

Harold and his men were perched on the hill looking down at the invading Normans when suddenly someone looked at the sundial and said, 'Hey, hang on a minute – it's nearly half past three; aren't we due a tea break?'

And while our boys sat and worked their way through a few tins of Teatime Assortment and downed flagons of the steaming hot brown stuff, William and his lot took over and made us all speak French. Dastardly foreign tactics.

Luckily, the speaking of French and the downing of *tasses* of *café* instead of tea didn't catch on with the majority of the population. And while the courtiers (French word) were happy to go along with it, the rest of us continued with our time-honoured traditions.

Perhaps it was enshrined in Magna Carta. Who knows? Have you read it lately? No, us neither. But somewhere in the small print there is probably a paragraph saying something like: 'It is the inalienable right of every Englishman (no politically correct stuff then about Englishwomen, of course) to partake of tea at the hour and in the manner of his choosing. The sound of England is the sound of the kettle whistling! Tea drinkers of the land unite! You have nothing to lose but your thirst!'

TV Dinners Do's And Don'ts

Do: place your dinner plate on a tray to prevent its heat from burning your legs.

Don't: try and do without either a tray or plate and just plop the hot meal straight on your trouser legs.

Do: cook your TV dinner properly.

Don't: sit sucking it straight from the freezer like a savoury ice lolly.

Do: make sure your dinner is piping hot when you start eating it.

Don't: try warming it up a bit more by sitting on it for a few minutes.

Do: set out your first course, dessert and glass of water on your tray.

Don't: try serving them all together on one plate.

Do: occasionally look away from the TV screen and down at your plate.

Don't: become so riveted by *The Weakest Link* that you accidentally cut up and eat half a drinks coaster in the belief that it is an over-dry beefburger.

Do: bring any condiments and seasoning you may require from the kitchen.

Don't: start rooting under the cushions to find discarded grains of salt or blobs of tomato ketchup to add to your meal.

Do: enjoy a tasty TV dinner while watching a television show.

Don't: enjoy a tasty TV dinner while being featured on a live broadcast.

The Wrinkly's Guide To Tea

When we wrinklies think of tea we don't think about green tea or Darjeeling or any of that other nonsense; we think of tea tea. In other words, good old British tea. Yes, all right, we know our wrinkly tea probably comes from Ceylon or whatever they call the place these days, but you have to be careful out there when ordering tea. So here's a little guide:

Darjeeling

This is sometimes known as the 'champagne of teas'. Cold, bubbly and expensive? No, thanks. About as appealing as the 'tea of champagnes'.

Earl Grey

In theory this should be all right – it's named after an Englishman, for goodness sake. But it's scented! Might be OK to dab behind your ears, but definitely not for drinking.

Green tea

Green? Anything the colour of cabbage immediately rings alarm bells. And you're not allowed to put milk in it? Or sugar? We didn't build an empire on that!

Lapsang Souchong

By the time you've got your tongue round that little lot you've probably died of thirst.

Amazing Tea Facts

There is an organization known as the United Kingdom Tea Council but unfortunately its members never get anything done because they are always on a tea break or in the toilet.

Some say tea originated in China 4,700 years ago but it may date back to before the evolution of man, as film is known to exist of it being consumed by chimpanzees – particularly ones running removal companies or competing in the Tour de France.

Tea comes from the shrub Camellia sinensis, which, unusually in the plant world, produces leaves covered in small, perforated paper bags.

Most people know that tea is made with hot water, milk and sugar. Julie Andrews in *The Sound Of Music* clearly had a different method of making tea, as evidenced in her repeated claim that it was 'a drink with jam and bread'.

Tea can be drunk hot or cold. If it is drunk cold, however, it will be spluttered out one second later followed by a cry of, 'Bloody hell! My tea's gone cold!'.

From the 1940s onwards the world was successfully dominated by a German called Adolf – Adolf Rambold, who invented the automatic tea bag packing machine in 1949.

Tea drinkers can be recognized because they have brown teeth and are always on the look-out for the nearest toilet.

Non-tea drinkers can be recognized because when you offer them a cup of tea they will say, 'No, thank you; I don't drink tea.'

What Your Choice Of Biccy Says About You

Psychologists can tell a lot about people by the way they write, what clothes they wear and even by how they eat their chocolate eggs, so it's no surprise to find they have now discovered that your choice of biccy also reveals something about you. The science of biccology is still in its infancy, but we can share some initial findings gathered by the University of Middle England.

Rich Tea

Otherwise known as 'the dunker's delight'. On the surface a rather dull and safe choice, but if you are a dunker it reveals that you like to live a little bit dangerously. Will the soggy half of the biscuit drop into the murky depths of your mug, never to be salvaged? Will you mount a rescue attempt? Will your last swig of tea be a dead biscuit sludge?

It also reveals you as a decision-maker. The split-second timing of when to remove your dunked biscuit from the tea without losing half of it is something that can only be accomplished successfully by a high-flying dunker.

Chocolate finger

This is the choice of a chocoholic in denial. Yes, it's chocolate, but it's so thin it can hardly be fattening, can it? No, not if you only have one: but when you scoff the entire packet at one sitting it's a different kettle of chips.

Ginger snap

This reveals you as something of a rebel. Yes, it does make my tea taste funny, but who cares? Bring it on!

Chocolate HobNobs

Fearless. You look the world right in the eye and say, 'If I'm going to eat biscuits, I'm going to have proper ones, with chocolate all over them, and damn the consequences!'

Highland shortbread from a tartan tin

You're cautious, and perhaps a little careful with the pennies (and that's not a racist jibe at Scotsmen, by the way) because in reality no-one buys these tins for themselves. They receive them as Christmas gifts and get them out on special occasions. It saves buying them, too!

Jammie Dodgers

You like to live on the edge – of the universe. Yes, they're Doctor Who's favourite biscuits, apparently. Basically, you're just a big kid, aren't you?

Not eating biscuits at all

You're still not safe from psychoanalysis; the biccologists will have you marked down as some thin-lipped puritan whose idea of excitement is repainting the front door, so you may just as well tuck in anyway.

Everything You Ever Wanted To Know About Biscuit-Dunking But Were Afraid To Ask

- Dunking a biscuit in a hot milky drink will release 11 times more flavour from the biscuit.

- It will also make it 11 times more likely that your biscuit will fall apart and land in a squidgy dollop on the floor.

- It is very bad manners to dunk your biscuit in your tea when in polite company.

- It is very bad manners when in polite company to dunk your biscuit in someone else's tea, even if you distract them first by getting them to look at something out of the window.

- It is very bad manners to dunk any bits of biscuit that you have already been chewing in your mouth for a few moments.

- It is very bad manners to pick up and eat a biscuit that you have dunked and which has fallen in a squidgy dollop on the floor.

- It is very bad manners to dunk your biscuit in someone else's tea, have it crumble into a squidgy dollop and then to try sucking it up out of their lap.

- It is very bad manners to try dunking your biscuit in someone else's drink when the drink is in their mouth.

- Despite the popularity of dunking biscuits, biscuits sold in a ready-dunked state have not proved to be great sellers.

- Biscuit-dunking addicts will begin to salivate if they are ever introduced to anyone with the first name Duncan.

Pacing Yourself Snack-wise

The wrinkly day should not be one long stuffathon. You've got to keep that waistline down, haven't you? But, based on recent research, the following has been found to be a typical wrinkly day:

6.30am	Wrinklies are early risers and need a cup of tea to start the day. Oh, go on, then: a couple of biscuits as well.
7.00am	You want another cup of tea already?
7.30am	Breakfast.
9.00am	Yet another cup of tea?
10.00am	It's been an age since breakfast and the hunger pangs are starting to kick in. A couple of biccies with another cuppa.
10.30am	The window cleaner has called for his money – better put the kettle on. It would be rude not to offer him a slice of cake too, wouldn't it? Oh, go on, then; twist my arm…
11.00am	Elevenses!
11.30am	Surely not too early for a little pre-lunch sherry?
12.30pm	Lunch.
1.00pm	A cup of tea to wash lunch down.
2.00pm	One of the neighbours has stopped by for a chat. Get the kettle on!
3.00pm	There's no name for this, but it's the afternoon equivalent of elevenses – 'Threesies'?
4.00pm	I don't know about you, but I'm gasping for a cuppa. Oh, and there's those homemade shortbreads to use up.
5.30pm	Better start thinking about dinner – glass of wine for the cook?
6.30pm	Dinner.
7.30pm	How about a snack while we're watching *Corrie*?
9.00pm	A spot of supper.
10.00pm	Cocoa.
3.00am	I can't sleep, so I'll just see what's in the fridge…

Snacks To Avoid At All Costs

Amateur armchair users will, of course, snack on anything, little realizing the pitfalls, perils and perplexities involved.

We wrinkly armchair users naturally approach the whole thing in a more professional manner, and like everything else in life, there is a right way of doing something and a wrong way of doing something: or, to be more precise, the wrong way, and the wrinkly way.

As you may be virtually living in your armchair you should treat it like a home, which means keeping it clean and tidy. So, for the edification of younger readers and those who have just joined the wrinkly fold, here are a few tips:

Exploding snacks

We don't mean 'exploding' as in ballistic missile, but some snacks come pretty damned close: meringues, for example. Oh, the humble meringue can look innocent enough, all pink or white, the blushing bride of high-street confectionery, but sink your gnashers in and there's a sudden explosion which covers your bifocals in sugary dust and gets right down your crevices. Many a wrinkly has found meringue crumbs down the sides of the cushions a fortnight after the last meringue was munched. One extreme incident reportedly left a pouffe unusable. Beware.

Anything bigger than your own head

Yes, pizza, we're talking about you. It's bad enough when the pizza has been decanted on to a plate and slips off one side as you try to hack into it with your knife, but if you're trying to eat it with your fingers out of the box it will be flopping around like a demented giant jellyfish and dripping that runny cheese all over your cherished upholstery without a care in the world.

Squidgy stuff

The thought of a nice cream-filled éclair to go with your afternoon cuppa is bordering on the exciting, but caution: food hazard ahead!

The loaded éclair is the AK-47 of afternoon snacks. Just picking it up will not only give you chocolatey fingers but can result in the entire front room being redecorated in cream.

Burgers packed with tomato sauce are similarly hazardous – especially those two-tier affairs that require one to open one's mouth to resemble the business end of the Mersey Tunnel. One gargantuan bite can result in a kaleidoscope of ketchup and mustard swirling in the air before you.

Crunchy stuff

Yes, we know that this would rule out a large part of the wrinkly daytime diet, i.e. biscuits, but the real villain here is the crisp. The combination of being greasy and prone to breaking into a million pieces is lethal.

Have you noticed that whenever you eat crisps you always find one crunched to smithereens under your bottom as you stand up? Then there is the 'last crumbs of the packet' scenario. This involves tilting the head back and pouring the last few reluctant morsels down your throat. In practice, it means covering yourself in crispy particles like a battered cod.

Dietary Disasters To Avoid

We have, of course, mentioned the messy and hard-to-handle snacks to avoid, but what about all those TV dinners, and maybe even TV breakfasts and lunches, that you consume while sitting in your armchair? Be careful out there!

The Greek meze

As you will know, this consists of a dozen or so different dishes on little plates, which may be fine when you're sitting at a table, but when you're sitting in your armchair with nothing more than a wicker tea tray with a picture of Windsor Castle on it this may be a problem. Avoid, unless you happen to be a professional juggler.

The Scandanavian smorgasbord

Any meal that incorporates the word 'gasbord' into its name has to be a non-starter. And when you come to the prospect of 20 or 30 dishes to balance on your lap… well, see above.

The Indian curry

Have you ever tried getting curry stains out of your armchair? Exactly.

Lobster

Tackling one of these beasts is akin to performing surgery. If your wrinkly other half is doing this properly you will be issued with a range of tools that will make the average NHS operating theatre look ill-equipped. Fine if he or she is prepared to stand at your side while you demand forceps, scissors, scalpels and all the rest, but spousal indulgence has its limits.

Barbecue

Yes, it is cold out on the patio, even in summer, but it is Not A Good Idea to try it indoors.

Moules marinière

Ever since that cheap alcohol jaunt to Calais you've been meaning to try this at home. How hard can it be? A big pot of garlic and wine, a few herbs and things and Bob's your *oncle*. Well cooking it's the easy bit: but a great steaming bowl of red-hot liquid swishing around on your lap will make you so nervous you won't be able to relax, and each time you accidentally drop one of the slippery little blighters back into the pot, as inevitably happens, it will splash your cherished chair with Gallic grease.

The Chinese takeaway

Firstly, you will find on arrival that the bag of goodies delivered by your friendly home delivery person will contain some unidentified little pots. These will contain various sauces which will be passed between you and your wrinkly partner to try. The law of averages says that in transit one of these will spill something of a garish hue on to your lovely lounge furniture.

Secondly, you will each want to 'just try a bit' of the other's food. Again, the passing of little boxes of this and that will probably end in tears.

Thirdly, the prawn crackers are the Chinese answer to the meringue, sending out a spray of dust everywhere when crunched.

Excuses To Crack Open The Alcohol Earlier Than Usual

As if you needed any! But there are unwritten rules in the world of the wrinkly, and one of these is that if the sun is not over the yardarm you are not allowed to pop a cork or trickle out a little of the hard stuff.

As it happens, you may not have the foggiest idea of where or what the yardarm is, but rules are rules, even unwritten ones, and you just have that guilty feeling that swigging the sherry at 10.30am is probably not on.

Therefore you need to have a ready list of excuses up your cardy sleeve just in case you get caught.

The celebration

It's well worth investing in a diary just for this. If it's not your second cousin once removed's birthday or Shrove Tuesday or some other legitimate excuse, you may find that it's Independence Day in Finland (December 6 if you want to know), or Constitution Day in Denmark (June 5), or, best of all, Veterans' Day in the UK (June 27).

Also, don't forget that the sun is over the yardarm somewhere in the world at all times.

Medicinal

Whisky for your throat, brandy for your stomach, egg-nog for a bit of protein... the inventive wrinkly will find a sound medical reason for opening almost any tipple you can name.

Longevity

The argument goes like this; I'm x years old, I've been drinking since I had adolescent acne and I'm none the worse for it. In fact, it's what keeps me going. In other words, I drink, therefore I am.

It needs using up

Well, you say, that half-bottle of brandy has been sitting there since Christmas so we might as well use it up. No, you concur, I know brandy doesn't have a 'drink-by' date, and I know it's still only December 29, but it's sitting there gathering dust...

Ooh, you little glugger!

Cultural reasons (1)

Now, if we were in France, you could argue, no-one would think twice about having a glass of wine before lunch. No, not with their cornflakes, admittedly, but that's only because they probably don't eat cornflakes for breakfast in France. *A votre santé!*

Cultural reasons (2)

It's well known that the Dutch always drink hock with doughnuts.

Keeping up with the Joneses

You think this is early? They have sherry in bed next door.

Ignorance of the time

If all else fails, simply put it down to a senior moment whereby you mistook the gloomy weather outside to be dusk and the TV breakfast bulletin to be the six o'clock news.

Things You Should Know About Downstairs Toilets

The downstairs toilet was invented by John Logie Wrinkly when he discovered that it wasn't possible to get to the upstairs toilet and back during a TV advert break.

The downstairs toilet is where most wrinklies would decide to shelter in the event of a nuclear attack.

Some downstairs toilets have sloping ceilings as a result of being fitted into a space under the stairs. This means that they can only comfortably be used while in a sitting or limbo-dancing position.

Things that wrinklies are obliged by law to keep in their downstairs toilet include a stock of old *Reader's Digests*, a bowl of pot pourri, a scented candle purchased from a garden centre, a small ceramic model of a lighthouse, a framed picture of an annoying relative and a sign with an amusing message written on it.

If a wrinkly leaves the downstairs toilet in too much of a hurry to get back to the TV, the light pull cord will be left banging against the toilet door and wall for several minutes afterwards.

Popular terms used by wrinklies to refer to the downstairs toilet include: the cosy cupboard, the reading room, the fortress of solitude, the department of philosophy, the temple of contemplation, the little house on the prairie, the air-lock, the observation turret, the confessional, the drop zone and the French embassy.

For people who live in bungalows, the downstairs toilet is known simply as 'the toilet'.

Chapter 10:
A Spot Of Housework

Of course, you can't sit in your comfy armchair all day doing nothing. No; there's housework to be done.

There are several reasons for doing housework. These include hygiene, improving your home's appearance and being able to find where the cat's got to under the piles of rubbish.

There are three things that need regularly cleaning up in a wrinkly's home: dust, dirt and rubbish. Dust is the substance produced when your wrinkly partner scratches him/herself. Dirt is what they leave on the carpet because they didn't wipe their feet when they came in, and rubbish is all your partner's worldly possessions that you haven't so far managed to sneak out of the house in a charity collection bag while they weren't looking.

Basically, there isn't a wrinkly alive who doesn't think their home would be made cleaner and tidier in an instant if they just got rid of their wrinkly partner. Unfortunately, it's often quite difficult to get these originators of rubbish to move either completely out of the house or, alternatively, into a specially-built kennel by the back door.

Many wrinklies are, of course, experts on cleaning. They have cupboards stocked with cleaning materials and know the best ways of managing every aspect of housework. It's this expertise that often leads them to assume a managerial role and stand barking instructions at their partner or some hapless lackey while they do all the cleaning for them.

These days, many like to use natural cleaning products and methods or, as they are known to wrinklies, cleaning products and methods which don't actually work. Wrinklies will, by contrast, usually choose cleaning products capable of killing 99% of all known germs, as well as a similarly high percentage of all life on Earth.

Wrinklies' homes will thus usually be gleaming, sparkling and will contain no living creatures other then those that make regular financial contributions towards the housekeeping. Any polished surfaces will be smooth, spotless and shining. This is because the house will largely be unoccupied, as its wrinkly occupants have to spend most of their time in hospital recovering from broken limbs after slipping over on their smooth, spotless, shining floors.

You should think about doing some cleaning every day: and, indeed, conscientious wrinklies will spend an hour or two each day doing just that – thinking about cleaning. Well, if just thinking about exercising results in you burning actual calories, shouldn't thinking about doing the housework have a similarly magical effect?

In fact, it may not be necessary for wrinklies to leave their armchairs to do the housework. After all, most of the mess that needs clearing up will be in the immediate vicinity of the wrinkly's chair, seeing as this is where the wrinkly spends most of his/her day.

Wrinklies can thus sit back and hoover, mop and dust in an arc around themselves, leaving a perfectly clean circular area around their chairs.

Wrinklies' Words of Wisdom
On Housework

If you spill something, the best time to clean it up is immediately... after you've finished shouting and swearing about it for five minutes.

Cleanliness is next to Godliness, but only in an extremely abbreviated dictionary.

The best time of day to get all your housework done is first thing in the morning... when your cleaner arrives.

Cleaning up stains and mess will provide you with a work-out... working out how to blame it all on your partner.

Never put off until tomorrow what you can bully your partner into doing today.

Tell your partner you've worked out a way to share the housework – they do the cleaning; you point out the bits they've missed.

Don't look on it as dust and dirt; look on it as naturally occurring insulation for your house.

Don't just brush the dirt under the carpet; the rug, the sofa and the occasional table can all be used as well.

If there's a mess in your house, draw up a big cleaning rota – then hide the mess under the rota.

Your house is not going to clean itself, so there's nothing for it; you're going to have to move.

Other people decorate their house in a minimalist style, you apply the same principle, but only to the cleaning.

Wrinkly Cleaning Techniques

The cleaning rota

This is a chart drawn up in a moment of insane optimism by whichever one of a wrinkly couple is going to end up doing all the cleaning on their own. The rota will list a series of items of housework and the name of which person in the house is going to perform this chore on which day.

If the rota also includes the names of any of the wrinkly couple's teenage offspring, then the person who drew it up should immediately be sent for psychiatric assessment.

Use the vacuum cleaner to do everything

Why bother with dusting or cleaning the windows when there are a range of different attachments on the vacuum cleaner? Wrinklies will be capable of flipping between these attachments like David Bailey swapping camera lenses as they move between vacuuming the stairs, the curtains, down the side of the sofa, dusting their knick-knacks and removing the fluff from their own navels.

Wrinklies should not, however, use the vacuum to suck up puddles of water or hoover the family pets each morning before they've had a chance to scatter their fur all over the house. Nevertheless, they always wonder about doing this, and this is why their pets look nervous whenever the vacuum cleaner comes out.

Remember, hoovering your pets is a cruel and terrible thing to do, particularly if attempted on animals whose waist measurement is less than the circumference of the vacuum cleaner extension hose (e.g. hamsters).

The spring clean

A thorough clean performed once a year in the spring. The theory is that you completely empty your house and put everything out in the garden. A few moments later there will be an unexpected spring shower and everything will get washed in the downpour.

Sweep all your rubbish under the carpet

This works for a while, but remember to stop when the height of your living room begins to be seriously affected. If there is no longer enough room for you to stand up once you've clambered up on to the carpet, it may be time to employ a cleaner.

Get a cleaner

Yes, the ideal way to get your cleaning done – get someone else to do it for you.

These days there is a range of companies who will come and do all the cleaning in a wrinkly's house. These enterprises have amusing names such as Molly Maid, Merry Maid, Maid For You, Maid For It or Maid A Bit Of A Mess Haven't We.

Many of these names seem to suggest a certain level of flirtatiousness surrounding the concept of the 'maid'.

Luckily, the cleaning companies involved sidestep any possible misunderstandings that might arise by sending out ladies who might better be described as 'matron' rather than 'maid'. Nevertheless, male wrinklies beware; do not get in the bath and ask your professional cleaner to give you a once-over with the cleaning cloth once they've finished the rest of the house.

Signs You May Have Left It Too Long Since Your Last Spring Clean

- You employ a cleaner and they arrive dressed in a biological hazard protection suit and mask.

- After a few days tidying your house, you have to call in a team of archaeologists to help with excavating the historical artefacts.

- Scientists discover a rare species of mini-beast living in your house and your living-room is officially declared a wildlife sanctuary.

- You uncover an elderly member of your family who everyone thought had died years ago sitting on a chair in the corner of your living-room.

- When you decide it's time to get up and get the cleaning things you realize you can no longer find the living-room door.

- You discover in the cupboard tcleaning products that are no longer available as they have now been banned under international chemical weapons agreements.

- You find you have cleaning products so old that they have started to go mouldy.

- Your cupboard of cleaning products looks like a museum exhibit depicting domestic life in the last century.

- Your vacuum cleaner is such an old model, it has to be plugged into the light socket.

- When you vacuum, the carpet starts changing colour and the room appears to get higher.

Wrinklies' Preferred Traditional Cleaning Materials

Lemons

Squeezed lemon juice can be used to clean the toilet, so if you drink nothing but lemon juice, presumably you will be able to clean your toilet during your normal natural visits.

Vinegar

Use vinegar to clean mirrors, windows etc. This will leave your house stinking permanently of vinegar and you feeling constantly that you must have chips for tea.

Bicarbonate of soda

Sprinkle this over your carpet. The white powder will deodorize your carpet but it will also make your guests think you suffer from terrible dandruff.

Denture cleaning tablets

You can clean the stains off all sorts of things using ordinary denture tablets. Why not install a large barrel next to your bed and leave all your cups, saucers, plates, clothes, shoes, the dog's bowl, etc. floating around in a fizzing mixture of dissolved denture tablets each night? Don't forget to throw your dentures in on top as well.

Tea tree and eucalyptus

These can be used as natural, environmentally-friendly disinfectants, and to make them even more environmentally-friendly, why not walk all the way to Australia to fetch them?

The Exciting World Of Vacuum Cleaners

Vacuum cleaners often used to be made by the Hoover company. This was quite a coincidence because, as everyone knows, the expression used to describe cleaning the carpet using a vacuum cleaner is 'doing the hoovering'.

The Hoover company was founded by Mr Henry Hoover. Hoover had gone into the vacuum cleaner business to try and escape the ridicule he received elsewhere for being a squat, red-faced little man with an oddly long, tube-like nose.

Hoover's slogan was: 'It beats as it sweeps as it cleans.' However, this caused confusion and many early Hoover users gave themselves hernias trying to pick up their vacuum cleaners in order to use them to beat rugs hanging up in the back garden.

Hoover cleaners featured a bag which caught all the dirt and dust from the carpet. A special indicator would tell the user when the bag was full by spraying a cloud of grey dust into his/her face whenever the cleaner was switched on.

Once the bag was full to bursting with dirt, hair and dust, it could be extracted from the cleaner and used as a nice new pillow at bedtime.

There were many designs of vacuum cleaner available, all of which required different types of dust bag. Wrinklies would thus end up with a cupboard or perhaps small annexe to their house entirely filled with vacuum cleaner bags which they had purchased only to find that they were the wrong sort.

These days, vacuum cleaners look like some kind of device from the film *Blade Runner*. They will come equipped with a range of different attachments which are know professionally as the brush one, the long, thin, pointy one and the one shaped a bit like Cherie Blair's mouth.

The Dyson vacuum cleaner was (again coincidentally)

invented by James Dyson. Dyson had become so fed-up with buying the wrong sort of vacuum cleaner bags that he decided to invent a machine which didn't need a bag at all.

The Dyson machine instead uses cyclone technology, and if you switch one on without the lid attached properly it will blow the roofs off every house in your street.

The Dyson cleaner collects all the dirt and dust from the floor in a transparent plastic canister. Wrinklies find it fascinating to watch this and see just how filthy their houses were. They will often call their wrinkly partner over and perhaps invite some wrinkly friends round as well to stand and admire all the detritus they have just vacuumed up, and in which they were wandering about quite happily a few minutes earlier.

Instead of throwing away a bag, the Dyson's wrinkly owner must take its plastic canister filled with dust out to the bin and empty it as though scattering the remains of a loved one.

The wind will inevitably change at this moment and the wrinkly will wander back into the house covered in a layer of grey dirt.

The Wrinkly's Guide To Traditional Cleaning Tools

The old-fashioned mop and bucket

Wrinklies know that you can't beat the old-fashioned floor mop and bucket. Yes, it's old, grey and a bit smelly, but so are many wrinklies. Not only is the mop a tool that has been tried and tested over centuries; it is also possible to put the end of an old mop on your head in order to pretend that you have a Rasta hairstyle.

An old pair of discarded pants

Wrinklies have long been the champions of reusing and recycling. Over the years, wrinklies have been able to afford many home improvements and expensive foreign holidays because of the money they have saved using discarded old pants instead of new cleaning cloths. Look at any wrinkly's front window and you will see a yellowy old pair of pants being rubbed this way and that against the glass – hopefully not while still being worn by their wrinkly owner.

Carpet sweeper

It's like a vacuum cleaner, but without any electricity. It brushes up the dust, which bounces around inside for a few minutes and then comes straight out again on a different part of the carpet.

Old-fashioned feather duster

Wrinklies can use these to torture their wrinkly partners by tickling them until they agree to clean the house. Alternatively, you could always chase a live chicken round the house and presumably they will do a bit of dusting as they run backwards and forwards along your mantelpiece.

The Wrinkly's Guide To Avoiding Housework

Try to pass off all accumulations of filth and rubbish in your home as pieces of conceptual art; if Tracey Emin managed to get out of cleaning her bedroom this way, so can you.

Get a fluffy pet that will hopefully pick up some of the dirt and transport it outside. If your pet doesn't pick up the dirt naturally, try applying a soluble, non-toxic glue. Any rubbish the animal brushes against will then be carried out and, once outside, washed off the animal's back by the rain.

Adopt minimalist décor throughout your house. Having no furniture in your home will mean that the dust and dirt will have nowhere to settle. You will also have nowhere to sit down, no telly to watch and will end up so bored you'll end up feeling like doing a bit of cleaning to pass the time.

Leave your front door unlocked when you go out in the hope that burglars will come in and steal all the rubbish.

Open your windows and doors in the hope the rubbish will be blown out of your house at least as far as next door's garden.

Play a game of 'Who can put up with all the mess for the longest time?' with your spouse – then once they've given up and have just finished cleaning and polishing the entire house, tell them, 'Ohhh! You needn't have done that! I was just about to do that!'

Odd Claims Made In Adverts For Cleaning Products

Kills 99% of all known germs

Yes, but the 1% it leaves wandering around the underside of your toilet seat could be a lethal superbug variant of bubonic plague.

Cleans in seconds

This will often be printed on the side of a bottle of cleaning fluid, but invariably this boast depends on the speed of the person who is doing the cleaning. The slogan should probably be expanded for wrinklies to instead read: 'Cleans in seconds, but if you're a wrinkly maybe give it an hour or two with a break for tea and biscuits'.

Environmentally friendly

Cleans bugger-all. It's the environment that makes things dirty in the first place, isn't it? The environment is the very thing you need your cleaning products to get rid of – not be friendly to.

Your money back if you're not 100% happy

Have you ever been 100% happy with anything? With this guarantee you could be entitled to your money back on everything that's ever happened to you in your life.

New and improved

A phrase coined to depress wrinklies who often feel neither 'new' nor 'improved'. And does anyone remember the manufacturer previously telling us that his product wasn't quite as good as it could be? No: but somehow he's now managed to make it 'new and improved'. Any old stock of the product left on supermarket shelves should now presumably be re-labelled 'old and ineffective'.

Leaves your hands soft

Hands aren't meant to be soft. They've got bones in the middle of them. If your hands are soft, you've got real problems and should phone for help immediately (although if you have got soft hands, picking up the phone and dialling may prove difficult).

Bang, and the dirt is gone

A controlled explosion seems a rather extreme way to do any sort of domestic cleaning. There would seem to be a genuine danger that, following the 'bang', not only would the dirt be gone but so would most of your house.

Loves the jobs you hate

Can this really be true? Have they invented a product that will not only help with your household cleaning but will also be overjoyed to fill in your tax return for you?

Makes your windows sparkle

Not only will your windows be clean; they will also threaten to dazzle and thus bring down passing aircraft.

Do the Shake n' Vac and put the freshness back

Ah! We all remember the Shake n' Vac lady. We can all sing every word of the Shake n' Vac song. We all do the little Shake n' Vac dance whenever we do the hoovering. And yet, ironically, none of us has ever once been tempted to buy a bottle of Shake n' Vac, or is even sure that the product is still generally available. How much does it cost companies to put their adverts on the telly?

The Wrinkly Guide To Removing Wine Stains From The Carpet

It can be annoying when you stain your living room carpet with red wine, but wrinklies know many traditional methods of stain removal. Of course, it would be easier if you hadn't spilt it in the first place, you clumsy, drunken old fool.

1. Use a cloth to mop as much of the stain as you can.

2. Now you've got a stained cloth as well.

3. Wash with soapy water.

4. No. We meant wash the stain with soapy water. Towel yourself dry and give the carpet a good scrub.

5. Well, that's helped spread the stain over a much wider area, hasn't it?

6. If you have spilt red wine, try pouring white wine over the stain. Now you've got two stains and you've wasted half a bottle of white wine as well.

7. Now pour half a tub of a leading brand of stain removal powder over the stain and leave to sink in for a few minutes.

8. Oh, look; now the stain stands out even more because it's been bleached bright white by the stain remover.

9. Better pour some more wine over it to try and turn it back the way it was.

10. Oh, never mind. Try hiding it under a rug instead.

Chapter 11:
A Bit Of Peace And Quiet

The wrinkly armchair should be a place of sanctuary, far from the madding crowd, even farther from the madding out-of-town shopping centre and, with a bit of luck, light years away from thudding discos, football hooligans and all the rest of the hoi polloi put on this earth to annoy you.

Within the comfort of your armchair you should find peace, tranquillity and escape.

But does it actually work out that way in real life? Is Donald Duck a duck? In reality you are plagued with interruptions, annoyances and disturbances from the moment your wrinkly bottom touches the cushion.

If it's not the telephone it's the doorbell, if it's not the doorbell it's the neighbours, and if it's not the neighbours it's… well, you name it.

Sometimes you truly believe that there's a conspiracy out there to deprive you of your peace of mind, not to mention your sanity.

You may doubt that the moon landings were secretly filmed in the Arizona desert, you may mock the notion that Kennedy was killed by the CIA, you may even pooh-pooh the idea that Elvis is alive and well and living in Grimsby and earning a good living as an Elvis tribute act but, as sure as eggs are breakfasts, you are often convinced that someone, somewhere doesn't want you to have a moment's peace.

In fact, they're probably watching you now.

'There he/she is – just walked into the front room with a newspaper and a cup of tea. Ah, picking up a pen, probably about to tackle the crossword – OK, start the road drill!'

Call us paranoid, but how is it that cold-callers only

phone when you're at home? When did you last come back from the shops to find a message on the answering machine saying, 'Ello, my name's Chantelle and I was wondering if you were interested in changing your gas and electricity supplier?'

Never. See – never happens, does it?

This can only mean one thing; they're watching the house. Or, maybe, in these technological times, they've fitted some monitoring device to your phone that alerts them when you go out.

And that bloke with the road drill; he could be in the pay of the cold-callers. As soon as you get back from the bingo he's on the blower to let them know it's safe to call with a once-in-a-lifetime offer.

Then there are your lovely neighbours. Whoever they are, they all suffer from the same mad impulse to saw wood at midnight or see if the volume control on the TV goes up to 11, or 'just have a few friends round' when you're looking forward to an early night.

You, of course, are the model of courtesy, responsibility and neighbourliness and wouldn't dream of such things.

If only there were more wrinklies out there.

Good Noise Versus Bad Noise

Not all noise is bad, though. The gentle boiling of a kettle, the satisfying crunch of a biscuit, the click of next door's stereo being turned off at 2am – lovely sounds one and all.

So let's not get too grumpy about noise; let's distinguish between good noise and bad noise. For example:

Good Noise	Bad Noise
The rustle of cellophane being taken off a new box of chocolates.	The crunching and masticating of your wrinkly partner scoffing them without offering one to you.
The friendly popping of the coffee percolator as it makes fresh aromatic coffee.	The moaning of your wrinkly other half saying it's your turn to clean it out.
The charming chirruping of birds outside, signalling that spring has finally arrived.	The twittering racket of birds who seem to have no idea that it's 4.00am.
The contented purring of your cat as it sleeps on your lap.	The contented snoring of your wrinkly partner as you wonder how the hell you're going to get them up to bed.
The crackle and spit of a real log fire in winter.	Your own terrified screaming as you wake up to find a log has fallen out and set fire to the rug.
One of your favourite records.	One of next door's favourite records.
The glug, glug, glug of the first alcoholic drink of the evening being poured.	The glug, glug, glug of your wrinkly partner polishing off the last of the bottle when it's too late to get fresh supplies.

Ten Obstacles To Achieving Peace And Quiet

Only ten? We blame the modern world. We may once have had rickets, the bubonic plague and hanging, drawing and quartering, but we didn't have noise, noise, noise, morning, noon and night.

Well yes, the people dying of the above-mentioned may well have made a bit of a racket with their wailing and gnashing of teeth and all that, but did they have spotty little Herberts racing around on mopeds that made a sound like a cat being neutered?

Did they have ice-cream vans patrolling the streets blasting out 'Popeye the Sailor Man' and sounding like a tone-deaf gibbon playing the vibraphone? Did they have to put up with people digging up the road every five minutes, or police helicopters clattering overhead or sirens going at all hours, or burglar alarms or car stereos pounding out that thump, thump, thump noise or...? See, now you've got us started. So, here are just ten:

Something indiscernible

You know how sometimes you suddenly become aware of perhaps a little ticking noise, or an intermittent squeaking, and you can't for the life of you work out what it is? *Very* annoying.

Loud banging

This is always accompanied by your wrinkly partner asking, 'What on earth are they *doing* next door?'

Doorsteppers

These people always call just as you've sat down with a tray of something nice to eat on your lap. How do they *know*?

Fireworks in June

It's not Guy Fawkes' Night; it's not even the Chinese New Year or Yom Kippur or any other discernible anniversary, but some clot deciding to let off his box of bangers – just for the hell of it.

Someone else enjoying themselves

Like most wrinklies, you're the life and soul of the party once you're on the right side of a bevvy or two, but when there's a bash going on next door and you're stone-cold sober it's very irritating.

Urban foxes

Now as much a part of city life as graffiti and charity shops, they somehow manage to make a sound like a baby being murdered.

Personal stereos

If they're 'personal', how come we can still hear them? The constant 'tsk, tsk' sound is, of course, us wrinklies complaining.

Lumpy cushions

OK, they're not noisy but they stand four-square between you and a nice relaxing sit-down. Grrr!

Teatime telephone callers

People still think it's cheaper to phone after six, so they call just as you're settling down to eat. Nice one, BT!

Your wrinkly other half

They mean well, but all the same...

How To Guarantee Peace

It's something that has eluded world leaders since the dawn of time, but what use is world peace anyway if your own living space is a cacophony of noise?

So, if you don't mind, we'll just leave world peace on the back burner for a little longer while we concentrate on the more pressing need for wrinkly peace.

And by golly, we need it. Isn't it strange that as you get older and find your hearing isn't quite what it was, you are at the same time acutely sensitive to noise? How does that work? The rustling of a crisp packet in the cinema, the ticking of the bedside clock, the distant barking of a dog – all guaranteed to have you crawling up the walls within minutes. But when your wrinkly other half says, 'Are you going to sit in that armchair all day?' you don't hear a dicky- bird.

And that's the first way to guarantee peace – by copping a deaf 'un. After a while, perhaps several hours, your wrinkly other half will give up and have a meaningful conversation with the dog.

But copping a deaf 'un doesn't stop the noise. What you need is a five-point plan:

- Problem: workmen outside. Whether they're digging the road or laying tarmac, they can't do it without making a racket. If it's not the road drills it's their dreadful portable radios blaring out a distorted cacophony that makes it sound as if they're tuned into Radio Dalek. Solution: make them a cup of tea. No workman will continue to work when there's a cup of char going. Not only that, they will then be putty in your hands when you ask them to turn the radio down a notch or ask for a loan of their ear defenders while they're drilling.

- Problem: next door's party is keeping you awake. Solution: simply go round and complain and you will be invited to the party. You can then drink the place dry and everyone will go home.

- Problem: noisy foxes outside. Solution: tie a chicken carcass to the bumper of your car. Drive at a speed slightly faster than a fox can run and lure them to somewhere several miles from your house. Cut loose the chicken carcass. Sorted.

- Problem: door-to-door salesmen. Solution: remove the 'Welcome' doormat from outside and paint a pentagram. Change your door number to 666. Fix your doorbell so that instead of making a ding-dong noise or playing 'Colonel Bogey' it blasts out a terrifying snatch of 'Carmina Burana' from *The Omen*. That should do the trick.

- Problem: telephone cold-callers. Solution: if they hear a normal answering machine message they'll probably call back. But if you simply change it to: 'Thank you for calling the prize hotline. Calls are charged at £35 a minute and may be recorded for training purposes', they shouldn't bother you again.

Songs You Won't Want To Hear On The Wireless

'Shout' – The Isley Brothers
'Cum On Feel the Noize' – Slade
'Say it Loud – I'm Black and I'm Proud' – James Brown
'The Bangin' Man' – Slade
'Turn It Up' – Busta Rhymes
'Bang Bang' – Cher
'Flash Bang Wallop' – Tommy Steele
'Thunder Road' – Bruce Springsteen
Anything by Girls Aloud
'Boom Bang-A-Bang' – Lulu
'48 Crash' – Suzi Quatro
'Ring Ring' – ABBA
'Ding Dong, Ding Dong' – George Harrison
'Keep A-Knockin'' – Little Richard
Anything by Wham!
'Boom Boom' – John Lee Hooker
'Shake, Rattle and Roll' – Bill Haley
Anything by Screaming Lord Sutch
'Crash! Boom! Bang!' – Roxette
'Smash It Up' – The Damned
'Scream' – Michael Jackson and Janet Jackson
'Shout To The Top' – The Style Council
Anything by Primal Scream
'Hell Raiser' – Sweet
'Party All Night' – Mytown
'We Will Rock You' – Queen
'If I Had A Hammer' – Trini Lopez
'Wham Bam' – The Candy Girls
Anything by Extreme Noise Terror
'War' – Edwin Starr
'Tommy Gun' – The Clash
'Shotgun Wedding' – Roy C
'Bomber' – Motörhead (in fact, anything by Motörhead.)

Wrinkly Activities That Require Absolute Silence

The wrinkly leads a complex life. If the wrinkly in his natural habitat were observed by Sir David Attenborough it would make a fascinating documentary. *The Grey Planet*, perhaps?

Those outside the wrinkly world have but the faintest idea of what wrinkly life is all about and how many wrinkly activities can only be performed in the strictest silence.

Walk into a wrinkly household during one of these activities and, by contrast, a Benedictine monastery would seem like a madhouse of cacophony and wild abandon.

Take reading the paper, for example. Most people like a little bit of peace and quiet while reading, but the wrinkly requires absolute silence. The merest audible breath from their wrinkly partner will disturb their concentration and send them into paroxysms of indignation.

At one time the noise-sensitive wrinkly could potter off down to the local library and read a whole host of newspapers and magazines in dignified peace, but not now. The place is full of youngsters sitting at computer screens, tapping away like death watch beetles and crunching and slurping on snacks, which officially are not allowed, but unofficially are probably tolerated in case the library is sued under human rights laws.

Then there are the more complex activities such as threading needles. The combination of dodgy eyesight and unsteady hands can make the threading of a needle the wrinkly equivalent of conquering Everest.

With tongue firmly lodged at one corner of the wrinkly mouth and thread and needle poised uncertainly in either hand, the wrinkly will attempt a union more complicated than the most intricate bit of repair work done outside the Apollo capsule in outer space.

That's one small step for anyone else, one giant leap for a wrinkly.

And then there is biscuit-dunking. The fine balance between dunking your Rich Tea biscuit to perfection and watching half of it drop off into the depths of your mug makes the work of a crane operator look like a doddle. If the non-dunking wrinkly partner should be fool enough to make a racket – such as dropping a pin, perhaps – during this delicate operation, they will know all about it.

Hair-plucking is another activity which requires the concentration of a chess grandmaster coupled with the 20/20 vision of a racing driver, two things that don't come naturally to the wrinkly.

We will draw a discreet veil over where the hairs to be plucked are located, but suffice it to say that if the wrinkly is safely locked in the bathroom, tweezers in hand, by the mirror, they will not appreciate their fellow-wrinkly banging on the door and demanding to know how much bloody longer they're going to be.

There are many other wrinkly activities that require absolute silence, so tread carefully – there's nothing more disturbing than a disturbed wrinkly.

People And Things You'd Like To Ban

Again, where do we start? How about the entire non-wrinkly human race?

Ooh, it's a selfish world out there these days. Oh, for the times when one could hear the gentle clip-clopping of horses' hooves instead of the vroom-vroom of the motor car: when one would hear the merry music of the birds singing instead of the wailing of car alarms: the melodious babbling of the brook instead of the endless babbling of TV presenters and radio 'disc jockeys'.

Still, we live in the modern world and we're stuck with it, so come the wrinkly wrevolution here are just a few people and things on our hit list:

'Deejays'

We blame the pirates. Remember when we had radio presenters who spoke in nice voices and wore bow-ties while reading the news? How did we know, when it was on the radio? Well you could just hear that they were wearing bow-ties. Then came along this new breed of 'deejays' – all Flower Power scarves and patchouli – and that was that. Shoot the lot of them.

Alarms

Car alarms, burglar alarms, smoke alarms, cooker alarms, alarms on mobile phones, alarm clocks, 'Warning: this door is alarmed'… you can't escape them. Wherever you go, your wrinkly eardrums are assaulted by bells, whistles, sirens, klaxons, electronic beeping and goodness knows what. Give it a rest. Or better still, give us a rest.

Chuggers

Or in plain English, charity muggers. Yes, you know: those irritating young people who stand in the middle of the high street wearing a bright red bib thing and holding a clipboard, asking if you'd like to arrange a monthly direct debit to their charity. Which wouldn't be so bad if they were giving up their free time for the charity, but they're getting paid for it! Anyway, we wrinklies are the ones who should probably be on the receiving end of any charitable dosh flying around, not the giving end.

Computers

Yes, we know they're wonderful and the World Wide Web was invented by an Englishman (hooray!), but for gawd's sake, do we have to encounter someone staring into one every time we go to the doctor's, the dentist's, the hospital and everywhere else and constantly asking for our postcode? Wrinkly says 'No'.

Mobile phones

If anyone under the age of 40 has to sit anywhere for more than five minutes, the first thing they'll do is whip out their mobile and start messing around with it. They're on them when they're walking, driving, cycling, on the bus, train or hoverflippingcraft.

Then there are those hands-free ones that are especially worrying. You see someone walking towards you, apparently talking to themselves and laughing. You think they've just escaped from a loony bin, until you realize they're on the phone. How did we ever manage without them? Very nicely, thank you.

Ten Things To Keep Your Spouse Quiet For Five Minutes

Hide their glasses somewhere in the house where they will never think of looking for them.

Tell them that you think you can hear next door having a fierce argument or enjoying a passionate embrace.

Act as though you've been greatly put out by something they've done and when they ask you what it is, tell them that if they think about it they'll know.

Pretend to be on the phone talking to a friend by holding the receiver to your head and occasionally saying 'Mmhm' or 'Oh yes' even though there's no-one on the line.

Ask them to go upstairs and look for the cat because you think it might have got stuck behind a wardrobe.

Tell them you can't remember if you renewed the TV licence last year so could they go and find it and check that it's up to date.

Adopt a secret identity, send them a saucy email message and they'll spend a few hours working on their reply.

Pretend that you've heard an intruder somewhere in the house and you both need to listen very carefully for any further strange noises.

Tell them somebody is going to each house in the road with a collecting tin so they must turn off the lights and keep very quiet.

Force-feed them a large, extra-chewy lump of toffee.

Chapter 12:
Time For Bed

And now it's getting late in the day and wrinklies must get up out of their armchairs and go up the stairs to bed. Ironically, in order to do this many wrinklies will first have to be woken up from their day-long snooze.

So as the sun sets on another day, it's time for a wrinkly's thoughts to turn to matters such as the meaning of life, the transience of existence and whose turn it is to make the cocoa tonight.

Another day has passed and a wrinkly can think back on all the events of the past 24 hours. What triumphs and tragedies have occurred today? What adventures and achievements can be looked back on? What prizes and surprises has the day brought?

A wrinkly is usually able to run through these questions in about one and a half seconds before making a final check through the TV listings to make sure that there isn't anything else worth watching on the box tonight.

Obviously the great questions of life are among the few things that wrinklies are still capable of running through at any sort of speed.

Nevertheless, there remain some important tasks that a wrinkly needs to accomplish before the blessed release of sleep. After all, those cushions on the sofa aren't going to plump themselves, are they?

Over the years, wrinklies will have built up a number of chores to be done last thing. Often they may take all night.

Most wrinklies like to make sure that their homes are nice and tidy before they go to bed.

Non-wrinklies often go to bed leaving a mess downstairs which they intend to sort out the next morning. This is a terrible mistake. If you leave your house in a mess, it can be very difficult the next morning to tell whether you have been burgled or not during the night.

Then, finally, it's time to sleep, perchance to dream.

Sleep remains a mysterious process, but possibly it helps us to rejuvenate our brains and bodies. If this is the case, many wrinklies will feel they've clearly not getting enough sleep and should increase their amount of slumber to around 24 hours a day.

Mammals, birds, reptiles and fish all sleep. Vegetation, rocks and young people do not: or, at least, not much.

Young people repeatedly refuse to go to bed at a reasonable hour. This reluctance to go upstairs and get themselves ready for bed is another example of just how lazy young people can be.

The times when wrinklies choose to go up to bed vary. Some wrinklies may even stay up all night. Their reasons for doing this will differ from those of young people. Maybe they're too tired to get up the stairs; maybe they fell asleep during *Countdown* and have only just woken up again.

Or maybe it's just that their stairlift has conked out and they're stuck downstairs for the night.

Telltale Signs It May Be Time For Bed

- You've feeling far too tired to get yourself ready for bed.

- You can't fit any more cocoa mugs in the washing-up bowl.

- The house is vibrating slightly with the sound of your wrinkly partner snoring away upstairs in bed.

- The TV programmes being broadcast on the BBC are all things that you've already seen but which now have a little person in the corner signing for the deaf.

- Everything being broadcast on every other TV channel now features constant swearing, graphic violence or nudity.

- The only people still walking by outside the house are now drunk and singing loudly.

- The dog is staring at you, wondering when you're going to finally vacate your nice warm chair for the night.

- The central heating went off hours ago and it's now getting so cold in the house that there's a danger of hypothermia if you don't get yourself to bed.

- Your electricity supply has now gone on to the cheap rate night-time tariff, so you'll save money when you use the stairlift to get upstairs.

- You've been sent into a hypnotic trance by the sound of the shipping forecast on the radio.

Excuses For All The Things You Didn't Manage To Get Round To Doing Today

Finding a cure for the world's most terrible diseases

OK, maybe you didn't manage to do this today, but then, as far as we know, neither did anyone else. Furthermore, there are some scientists in the world who are being paid large amounts of money and given as much lab equipment and as many test tubes as they could want to help encourage them to do exactly this, and yet, to date, they don't seem to have achieved any more than you have. And as a wrinkly you've probably had some of the world's most terrible diseases – well, the common cold, at least – and so far you've managed to get over them as best you could. Perhaps in the end it will be you who provides a cure for the world's most terrible diseases by virtue of your incredible natural wrinkly immunity and powers of recovery. Well, let's hope so.

Winning the Nobel Prize

The first excuse is that they weren't giving any out today. Secondly, you can argue that when the day comes that they give out Nobel Prizes for doing the gardening, housework or the Daily Mail Quick Crossword, you will surely be top of the Nobel committee's list for consideration. Better book your flight to Oslo now.

Saving the world from global warming

The world could all come and sit in your back room with you. It's usually quite chilly in there when the heating isn't switched on.

Winning the lottery

Maybe you didn't win the lottery today, but we wrinklies have more chance of scooping the jackpot than others. Just keep changing your numbers each week. Eventually, as a result of wrinkly longevity, you'll work through every possible combination and maybe even win £10.

Running 100 metres in 10 seconds

Admittedly you would find difficulty in doing this unless you were going down a particularly steep incline. However, athletes who manage to run 100 metres in 10 seconds are all youngsters. Ten seconds is proportionately a larger percentage of their total lifespan than it would be for any of us wrinklies. This means that running 100 metres in 10 seconds when you're 20 is the equivalent of doing it in 20 seconds when you're 40.

By the time you're 60, you only have to cover the distance in 30 seconds. But where are our gold medals and places in the sporting world records?

Admittedly, by the time you're 80 and have an entire 40 seconds to travel 100 metres, you may have difficulty in moving that far at all. I suppose it will still count if you do it using your mobility scooter.

Writing your novel

You've been working on finding a cure for the world's most terrible diseases, you've covered 100 metres in the equivalent of 10 seconds, you're on your way to winning a Nobel Prize for solving the *Countdown* conundrum each day, and people expect you to write a novel as well?

A Comparative Table Of Night-Time Activities Engaged In By Young People And By Wrinklies

What Young People Do Each Night	What Wrinklies Do Instead
Spend the entire night going from pub to pub.	Spend the entire night going from bed to toilet.
Get off their heads on cocaine.	Get off their heads on cocoa.
Go to a club.	Go to the Darby and Joan Club.
Party till they drop.	Drop.
Binge session.	Bingo session.
Drop a few tabs.	Drop their prescription.
Update their Facebook status.	Update their library book renewal status.
Have an intimate liaison with a complete stranger.	Have an intimate liaison with a complete stranger, but only because it's the carer sent to help undress them and put them to bed.

Go to bed with the first person they meet that night.	Go to bed with the only person they've seen all day (i.e. their wrinkly partner).
Don't get to bed until dawn.	Don't get to sleep until dawn because of all the young people passing by outside who haven't gone to bed until dawn.
Dance themselves dizzy.	Make themselves dizzy by standing up a bit too quickly.
Go to A&E after doing something wild and crazy.	Go to A&E after accidentally tripping over the cat.
End up completely exhausted after another night of wild abandon.	End up completely exhausted but with much less effort or financial outlay.

Other Things You Could Do Instead Of Going To Bed

Going to a dance

What could possibly go wrong with a group of wrinklies gyrating round on a polished surface in a confined area? Yes, any such event will be destined to include more tumbling over than a world record attempt involving dominoes. So if you go to a wrinklies dance, don't forget your camcorder. You could make a small fortune selling any footage you take to *You've Been Framed*. And there'll be no trouble getting home afterwards. After the dance, a fleet of ambulances will have been pre-booked to take the revellers away.

Going to a pub quiz

This is a popular activity for wrinklies who will, by this stage in their long lives, have accumulated a vast array of general knowledge, a small amount of which they will still be capable of remembering. Wrinklies may have to make a few minor adjustments in their vocabulary to understand the nature of particular rounds in the quiz. For example, when the quiz master announces a round on 'ancient history', to wrinklies this will mean 'history'; when he announces a round on 'history', to wrinklies this will mean 'current affairs' etc.

Going to the theatre

Many theatres now put on shows specially suited to wrinkly audiences and regularly present a mix of comedies, dramas, interesting talks and musical performances: or, in other words, exactly the same sort of thing that you can sit at home and watch on television.

Going to a pop concert

Many revival tours now exist, showcasing pop stars from years gone by. Not only will this be a rare opportunity for wrinklies to hear some nice old tunes that they recognize; it may also be their only chance to see people older than themselves who are still in regular employment.

Watch out, though, if you go to see an old pop group which no longer features all the original members. If you are in any doubt as to which of the band are the originals, they will be the ones sprouting grey hair from every orifice, who have to to be helped on by a nurse and who have a commode next to them on stage during the performance.

Having all your wrinkly friends round for a party

Why should it only be young people who throw parties for no apparent reason?

A party with all your wrinkly friends will, however, differ from a young people's party in several important respects.

Firstly, it will be a lot quieter and there will be fewer drugs involved, unless you include joint pain medication.

Secondly, it won't be the sound of the latest rave anthem that gets everyone worked up but a discussion of pensions or the cost of petrol: and finally, there will also be no problem in getting the last stragglers to leave in the early hours of the morning. In fact, the opposite problem may exist, and it may prove difficult to get anyone to stay much later than 9.30pm.

What To Do If Your Stairlift Breaks Down Halfway Up The Stairs

This is potentially disastrous. It's like thinking you were going up to heaven and then finding out halfway that you've been condemned to purgatory.

It's also particularly awkward if the stairlift is your only means of getting up the stairs. If you are, in fact, perfectly capable of getting up to bed under your own steam but just decided to have a stairlift fitted because you're a bit lazy, you will receive less sympathy when you are discovered the next morning halfway up the stairs.

Otherwise, the situation may be considerably less amusing. Nevertheless, it may give you a moment to consider adding the following to your 'to-do' list:

- Compose a strongly-worded letter to the man who serviced your stairlift just a few days earlier.

- Compose a similarly strongly-worded letter to the manufacturers of your stairlift, particularly if it turns out that it has stopped working because it requires a small battery to be changed every few months.

- Make sure that in future you don't venture up the incline without some means of summoning help, preferably by shouting to another wrinkly inhabitant of the household to come and give you a shove to get you moving again.

- Get a hotline number for your stairlift repairman, who will henceforth guarantee to come and carry you up the stairs if the machinery fails.

Things To Do Before Finally Going Up To Bed

Before going up the little wooden hill to bed (or, for more elderly wrinklies who have had stairlifts fitted, up the funicular railway that runs up the little wooden hill) there are a few jobs left to perform:

Plump the chair cushions ready for the morning; for many wrinklies this may be the most physical activity they have had all day.

Check the cat or dog doesn't need to go out (you don't need to do this if you don't own a cat or dog.)

Put out the bin for collection the next morning; if you are a wrinkly you will probably have done this by 3.30 in the afternoon.

Make sure the front and back doors are locked; burglars who come and try your doors during the night will then immediately give up when they find them locked.

Check the smoke alarm isn't working; if it goes off in the night you'll have the dickens of a job getting back to sleep afterwards.

Switch off all the lights, but not the one on the landing before you've got up the stairs, or you may fall all the way down again.

Switch off all other electrical appliances in the house, not including any life support equipment required by you or your wrinkly spouse.

Put the car in the garage; don't try doing this if you're feeling a bit drowsy or you may end up with your car parked in your dining-room.

What The Time You Go To Bed Says About You

8.00pm	This is a bit early, isn't it? Was it really worth your while getting out of bed today?
9.00pm	Once the evening's second episode of *Coronation Street* has finished there's nothing worth staying up for.
Five minutes after the central heating goes off	You don't like to be cold, do you?
10.30pm	In terms of times at which to go to bed, this is the equivalent of the missionary position.
11.05pm	If you are a wrinkly male, I hope you haven't stayed up to have a crafty peek at the adult channels that start broadcasting at 11.00pm.
11.59pm	You were traumatized as a child by the story of Cinderella and now do not dare to stay up past midnight.
12.01am	You had to stay up to video something off the TV starting at midnight but weren't sure whether you should have set the day as today or tomorrow.

12.45am	You refuse to go to bed until you have stood while the National Anthem plays at the end of Radio 4's broadcasts for the day.
12.48am	Not only do you have to hear the National Anthem; you can't resist listening to the shipping forecast either.
1.00am	You are a wrinkly wild child living life on the edge. Either that or you had an over-strong cup of coffee at some point in the evening.
2.00am or later	Wow; are you trying to set some kind of wrinkly world record or what?

Frequently Asked Questions About Wrinklies

Do you have to be old to be a wrinkly?

No, but it's best not to be too young before you become a wrinkly, because otherwise it looks a bit weird. Nevertheless, these days young people are clearly desperate to become wrinklies, as the popularity of sunbeds and tanning salons surely testifies.

Why are wrinklies so wrinkly?

Wrinklies are covered in wrinkles because of a lifetime enduring the stress and anguish caused by their offspring, their wrinkly partners, young people, work colleagues, shop assistants, the government, representatives of the local council, call centre staff, door-to-door salesmen, drivers, cyclists, pedestrians and the rest of humanity in general. If you aren't covered in wrinkles after a few years, you're either extremely tolerant or extremely unobservant.

Are all wrinklies wise with age?

Yes. And even if they aren't, they speak so slowly that whatever they say will sound rich with profundity even if it's just, 'These chips taste a bit funny.' Generally, however, wrinklies are famed for their wisdom because they spend so much of their time quietly cogitating – hence the expression 'old codger'.

Why do wrinklies move so slowly?

Because they've done everything there is to do at least once before, and so whenever you see a wrinkly doing anything, as far as they're concerned it'll be some sort of slow-motion action replay.

Why do wrinklies all dress the same?

It's a bit like in *Star Trek*. The cult sci-fi show showed us that in the future everyone would dress in the same basic outfit. Wrinklies have been around so long that as far as they are concerned they are now living in an amazing science fiction-style future. Thus wrinklies all wear the same outfits as one another. For some reason, however, wrinklies have opted for beige anoraks and slacks rather than the brightly coloured skin-tight space suits favoured by Captain Kirk and his chums... but perhaps that's just as well.

What are the seven signs of ageing?

Wrinkles, liver spots, more wrinkles, a beige anorak, wrinkles across your existing wrinkles, forgetfulness and... I can't remember the seventh one.

Why don't wrinklies use more skin-rejuvenating cream?

This is what we look like *after* using skin-rejuvenating cream. If we didn't we would look like something from *The Curse Of The Mummy's Tomb* and would crumble every time we bent over.

Why does wrinklies' skin bruise so easily?

Because young people are so flipping clumsy.

Are any anti-ageing products really effective?

Look on us wrinklies and despair!

What is the most effective way to avoid wrinkles?

Not being old.

Last Thoughts On The Wrinkly's Armchair

Before switching off the TV and the living room light and going up the stairs to bed, spare one last thought for your armchair.

Is the armchair not the wrinkly's truest friend of all?

Which of your other friends would bear your weight from dawn till dusk each day?

Which of your other friends would allow you to sit right on top of them without even being asked first?

Which of your other friends would allow you to gradually cover them and fill them with discarded crumbs from every meal and snack you consume?

Which of your other friends would sit there patiently day after day and never once mention that they cannot see the television because you keep parking your big fat behind right in their way?

Which of your other friends would allow you to leave such a deep and well-defined imprint of your buttocks all over them?

Which of your other friends would sit downstairs all night without the heating on, just waiting until the moment when you come down in the morning to do it all again?

Which of your other friends would do all these things and never once complain or make a comment about the state of your personal hygiene? Only your trusty armchair.

Although on the other hand, you've probably not tried doing many of these things with any of your other friends.

Glossary

A selection of words and phrases associated with the wrinklyverse.

World of leather
Any building, housing complex or other setting used exclusively by wrinklies.

The domino effect
An all-wrinkly dancing event.

Maracas
A wrinkly couple who have each recently consumed their prescription pills.

Dodo's toes
What wrinklies have round their eyes rather than crow's feet.

Life support system
Kettle, biscuit tin, television.

BOF
If a wrinkly is described as a bof this is not because they are balding, and thus resemble disgraced TV presenter Frank Bough. Instead, it means they are a Boring Old Fart.

Popemobile
A wrinkly's mobility scooter.

Egg-cosy
Woolly hat used by a bald wrinkly.

Rust
Wrinkly's dandruff.

Grecian 2000
Hair product used by wrinklies since their youth in the days of Ancient Greece.

Coffin-dodger
Either an abusive term for a wrinkly or, quite literally, a wrinkly who has almost managed to get run over during a funeral procession.

Boring people remote control mute switch
A hearing aid.

Ouija board
Online social networking site for wrinklies.

Crazy paving
Particularly deep wrinkles.

Draught excluder
A wrinkly who has fallen over in the hallway.

Nobbly bobbly
A wrinkly wearing an old acrylic jumper.

Spec-lace
Glasses worn on a string round the neck.

Linen gazetteer
A wrinkly's drawer full of old tea towels, each depicting landmarks from a different holiday location around the world.

Bag for life
Abusive term used by elderly men to refer to their wives.

Afterword

Well, wrinklies, the end is near and so you peep out of the final curtain to have a last check on what the neighbours are getting up to.

So now you have read through *The Wrinklies' Armchair Companion* from one end to the other.

Or at least you've flicked through it to find the good bits.

Or maybe you've just flicked through it.

Anyway, at least the reading and/or flicking is now over. You've finally got to the end. Congratulations. It's a bit like having run a marathon or reached the summit of a mountain, isn't it? Feel free to fashion a medal or small trophy to award yourself.

Now you are sitting there in your armchair, brushing your hair back into place (after flicking through the pages too quickly and causing a gust) and thinking thoughts such as:

'Thank goodness that's over', 'It was funny in bits, but overall I didn't quite get the plot', 'I can't believe I've just been sitting here in my armchair reading a book about sitting in an armchair', 'There's ten minutes of my life I'm not going to get back again', 'To whom should I send my letter of complaint?', 'That was the most fascinating in-depth study of wrinklies and their armchairs I have ever read, and I've read plenty!', 'Right! – now on to *The Brothers Karamazov*!' and/or 'I can't believe I'm still awake after reading all that.'

If you are still awake after reading all that, don't forget this book is liberally sprinkled with magic wrinkly sleepy dust. At least, that's the excuse that the publishers gave to the customs officers when they were bringing copies of the book into the country.

Just wave the book over your pillow to release the magic wrinkly sleepy dust and it will help you get to sleep. If your wrinkly partner finds you doing this, however, they may presume that you have gone loopy and will thus have you committed to a secure unit – the padded walls of which will also help you relax and get to sleep.

So either way – happy days!

Good night, wrinklies!

PS: If you have been affected by any of the issues raised during the course of this book you might like to call our helpline number where you will be able to speak in confidence to a specially-trained advisor.

Hopefully, however, none of the issues raised in this book will have affected you too much and you will have been left largely untraumatized by any of the details of cushion-plumping, snack items and downstairs toilets.

If you have been affected, though, we regret to inform you that there is bad news – we don't actually have a helpline.

If you have been affected by the news that those responsible for the production of this book have failed to provide a helpline number, please call the helpline number...

And then call us and let us know what it is.

Thank you.